Measuring Emotional Intelligence

Measuring Emotional Intelligence

The Groundbreaking Guide to Applying the Principles of Emotional Intelligence

by

Steve Simmons and John C. Simmons, Jr.

THE SUMMIT PUBLISHING GROUP
ARLINGTON, TEXAS

THE SUMMIT PUBLISHING GROUP
One Arlington Centre, 1112 East Copeland Road, Fifth Floor
Arlington, Texas 76011
summit@dfw.net
www.summitbooks.com

Printed in the United States of America.

01 00 99 98 97   5 4 3 2

Library of Congress Cataloging-in-Publication Data

Simmons, Steve, 1957-
    Measuring emotional intelligence : the groundbreaking guide
      to applying the principles of emotional intelligence / by
      Steve Simmons and John C. Simmons, Jr.
      p. cm.
                                                Includes index.
    ISBN 1-56530-268-0
    1. Emotions. 2. Emotions—Measurement. 3. Emotions and
      cognition. 4. Emotions—Social aspects. I. Simmons, John
      C. (John Castle), 1921-1988. II. Title.
    BF561.S555 1997
    152.4—dc21   97-33879
                                                   CIP

Cover design by Paul Perlow
Book design by Michael Melton

Contents

Acknowledgements

I would like to give credit to my father and coauthor, John C. Simmons, Jr., for originally identifying the specific areas of emotional intelligence (which he called character) in the early 1970s. He also: created the Simmons Personal Survey, which accurately measures the thirteen areas of emotional intelligence; wrote and taught our first seminars; and set up Simmons Management Systems (a national organization of business consultants, counselors, and organizational leaders). John Simmons passed away in September, 1988, but his vision still guides our organization, and his accomplishments continue to help others.

Thanks also go to my mother, Jill Simmons, for computer programming the Simmons Personal Survey. For twenty-six years, her work has made it possible for others to take the Survey and to receive computer evaluated results. She continues to make it easier to take the Survey, to return results faster, and to improve the information that is received. Jill also has been responsible for the automation of many of our organization's accounting functions.

I would like to express appreciation to my sister, Bonnie McAdams, for her help in editing this book and for seventeen years, her consistent commitment to managing the financial aspects of Simmons Management Systems. She also has edited and written in our monthly newsletter and has managed those who process our Surveys.

Our authorized Associates who have been our representatives in every state of this country are deserving of credit for helping their clients to hire better employees and to develop emotional intelligence in others. Many of these Associates have provided interesting stories and valuable instruction that have been used in our book.

Thanks to my wife Cheryl, who has been so supportive of my work during our nineteen years of marriage, and who has helped to professionally proof this book. Also, thanks to my three children, Mark, Paul, and Scott, who were particularly understanding of the time I had to borrow from them to research and write the book.

Last but not least, thanks to Len Oszustowicz, David Gavin, Bill Scott, Dee Richardson, and everyone at the Summit Publishing Group who, by applying their professional skills, have made this book so entertaining and beneficial to the reader.

Section One

Introduction

■ Measuring Emotional Intelligence

Daniel Goleman, in his best-selling book *Emotional Intelligence* has soundly proved that emotional intelligence is the single most important factor for personal adjustment, success in relationships, and in job performance.

Now, Measuring Emotional Intelligence, which is based on twenty-six years of research, takes the next step by giving *you* the keys to:

Measuring emotional intelligence in yourself and in others.

Emotional and behavioral strength.

Success in relationships.

Success in job performance.

Organizational success.

■ What You Will Learn in This Book:

Discover the dynamics of emotional and behavioral development.

You will understand yourself and others better as you begin to recognize the specific facets of emotional intelligence. You will learn a great deal about people and why they behave as they do.

We will show you how to build emotional intelligence in yourself and in others by demonstrating the general laws that govern growth and by detailing hundreds of specific growth-producing strategies.

You will learn about your own emotional characteristics and how they affect your job performance. You will have the opportunity to compare your traits to your specific job and to make quality decisions which will improve your job performance.

You will learn how to effectively relate to a wide variety of people such as friends, customers, your manager, and others. We give you strategies for successfully relating to the twenty-six specific types of people that exist.

Couples can learn how to understand each other and to work better as a team. You will see which characteristics are compatible, which cause conflict, and how to solve the conflicts.

Parents can learn how to be more effective in preparing their children for success.

Teachers can become more effective in stimulating learning and in managing the classroom.

Job seekers can learn about their personal traits and determine which jobs best suit them.

Managers and executives of organizations, spanning all industries, will find a way to hire more productive employees, develop employees, build productivity, increase sales, and to dramatically decrease employee related costs.

Professional counselors will find help in dealing with the psychological, relational, and job-related needs of their clients.

Measuring emotional intelligence will also help many business consultants who want to have an edge in helping companies select, place, develop, train, promote, and outplace employees.

Now, get ready to read and receive some of the most helpful information you will ever find.

Chapter 1

What Is Emotional Intelligence?

What's your IQ? Like most of us, you probably know the answer along with your SAT or ACT score and your high school rank. Simply put, IQ (which stands for intelligence quotient) measures how well a person does on a particular intelligence test. The test usually measures cognitive functions such as vocabulary, information for facts, short-term memory, verbal reasoning, eye-hand movement, nonverbal reasoning, and the ability to learn new relationships.

These tests do have some moderately strong ability to predict academic performance. The problem is that during the past fifty years, experts and laymen alike have relied too heavily on IQ scores to predict things like job performance and general adjustment in life. In reality, IQ does not strongly relate to these aspects of life, although it is of some importance. Many people who score low on the IQ tests succeed very well in life, while many of those who have high IQs underachieve.

Clearly, then, there are other factors besides IQ that determine success in the major tasks of life. For twenty-six years, our organization, Simmons Management Systems has studied and measured these other success factors. As early as 1970, we called them character. By 1975, we had discovered the thirteen major facets of character which relate to success in life and had developed a highly valid and reliable way to measure them.

These areas are Emotional Energy, Stress, Optimism, Self-esteem, Commitment to Work, Attention to Detail, Desire for Change, Courage, Self-direction, Assertiveness, Tolerance, Consideration for Others, and Sociability. We will fully describe these characteristics throughout this book.

In 1990, Peter Solovy and John D. Mayer called similar values "emotional intelligence." This term was used to directly contrast with the term "intelligence." Since 1990, many people have exchanged the words "emotional intelligence" for "character," although the two words describe the same thing. The term EQ stands for emotional quotient and refers to a person's level of emotional intelligence. Note that in this book we will use the words character and emotional intelligence interchangeably.

In 1995, Daniel Goleman, aware of the lack of knowledge by the general public about the subject, wrote a book called *Emotional Intelligence*. In the book, Goleman describes some of the types of emotional intelligence and shows how they have been proved by many research studies to be more significant than IQ in the areas of emotional health, relational success, and job performance. He also does a good job of summarizing research showing that like IQ, emotional intelligence is a function of the brain.

While Daniel Goleman shared much valuable information with the public about how important emotional intelligence is, and about how it relates to brain functions, there are three absolutely vital areas still to be addressed.

Precise Measurement of Emotional Intelligence. Without proper measurement of emotional intelligence, you cannot know which areas are sound and which need improvement, which are compatible with others and which are not. You must know the state or condition of something before you can suggest what needs to be done for improvement.

The Full Range of Emotional Intelligence. While others have discussed up to five aspects of emotional intelligence, our research shows that there are thirteen distinct areas.

Application. There is a need to teach how to relate to others based on emotional intelligence, how to develop emotional intelligence, and how to apply knowledge of emotional intelligence to the world of work.

In this book, we will go well beyond where others have left off. We will, therefore, describe all of the characteristics involved in emotional intelligence. Second, we will demonstrate how to precisely measure emotional intelligence. Third, we will discuss in detail how to build success through knowledge of emotional intelligence.

The stories of real people discussed in this book will quickly give you a good idea of what EQ is and of its effect on both job performance and in personal relationships. These stories are true. Names and some identifying information have been changed to protect the identity of the individuals.

■ Poor EQ Fit Causes Job Failure

Robert did very well in elementary school and in high school. He also excelled through four years of college, studying business. During college, he worked preparing food and running the cash register at a fast-food restaurant where he excelled. After graduating from college, the restaurant put him into its management training program. Being very intelligent, he rapidly learned the procedures necessary to be successful as a manager, and after just five months, he was promoted to full manager.

By all normal predictors, Robert was on his way to succeeding in restaurant management. Everyone who knew him was certain that he would do well. He was in excellent health, good looking, and highly intelligent; he had mastered the technical knowledge of the job, was interested in the work, and had support from all who knew him.

Yet, after being a manager for only a few months, Robert was failing. The results of store inspections by his supervisor were poor. Sales were down. Customers complained about the quality of the food, about the slowness of delivery, about the lack of cleanliness in the restaurant, and about the treatment they received from the employees. The company tried to tell Robert what they believed he was doing wrong, but the problems continued and even worsened. Predictably, the company was considering firing Robert.

So what went wrong?

While Robert had much going for him, he did not possess the correct degree of certain characteristics needed in a management job. First of all, he was not assertive enough to instruct and to direct his employees. When they performed poorly, he couldn't confront them to quickly correct performance. Only those employees who naturally had good work habits were performing acceptably. The rest of them were getting away with murder.

Because Robert wasn't decisive, he couldn't confidently solve these problems. As a result, problems persisted and even worsened. Because he didn't have enough assertiveness and decisiveness, and because he was very hardworking, Robert's solution to each problem was to do the work himself. He was putting in an incredible number of hours trying to make up for what others didn't do. And to make matters worse, Robert was clueless—he felt that he was doing a good job and that everything was working out. This was because of his excessively high self-esteem and optimism.

■ Good EQ Fit Leads to Job Success

Just as poor character fit can lead to disaster, having the right character for the job can lead to excellent job performance (assuming normal intelligence, appropriate experience, etc.).

After measuring Robert's EQ with the Simmons Personal Survey, we scheduled a meeting with him and his direct supervisor. During the meeting, we discussed the character traits that helped him on the job such as his commitment to work, his attention to detail, his positive attitude, and his consideration for others. As each area was discussed, we asked Robert to give examples of how these positive attributes were demonstrated on the job.

Then we discussed the character areas that did not fit the job, such as low assertiveness, low decisiveness, a tendency toward perfectionism, and being so positive that he overlooked problems. At this point in the meeting, Robert began to have difficulty. He couldn't recognize any of his "negative" characteristics. This was because, as our instrument indicated, he had excessively high self-esteem that protected him from feeling inferior.

During the last half of the meeting, as much data as possible was used to show Robert what actually was happening on the job and how that performance related to his character. Still, during the interview, Robert couldn't quite break through to accurately see himself. For about two weeks after the interview, Robert thought of little else besides what was discussed in the meeting. He didn't sleep much, and he began to have disturbing dreams.

Finally, after wrestling with these issues, Robert was able to see the truth about himself. With a better understanding of his EQ, he then began to follow the direction that had already been given to him in the meeting. He had been instructed to be clear and direct in giving instructions to his employees. When employees would make an error or purposely underperform, Robert was supposed to discuss this with the employee and, when necessary, apply discipline. He had been instructed to make it his job to delegate responsibility. His new definition of success involved his people doing their jobs well—not Robert doing their jobs well. He had been instructed to take the risk necessary to make his own decisions about people problems and about operational needs such as getting maintenance on a machine.

Once Robert understood his EQ, saw the problems, and made the commitment to change, he began to perform up to expectations. Even though he was now behaving and performing differently, it took him a month or two before he felt confident, assertive, decisive, etc. Finally, though, his feelings caught up with his behavior, and he actually became a very different and more successful person.

At first, others wondered what had happened to Robert. There was even some resistance to letting him be different than he was. Yet, through consistent daily practice, everyone saw and accepted the new Robert. By the end of five months, he was recognized as being the best manager in the entire restaurant franchise. We also administered the Personal Survey to him again and were able to see all of this progress in his EQ scores.

Just as amazing is the fact that Robert's success continued to grow. The company promoted him into higher management positions and then into executive positions. Today, Robert is very successful in his role as president of another large company.

Robert had originally failed because he didn't have all of the character traits needed for his job. Robert's career choice was doomed to fail because he didn't compare his emotional intelligence to the requirements of his chosen career. Hiring without proper EQ assessment resulted in failure. Training that didn't include attention to character was incomplete. Promotion without EQ assessment was unsuccessful. Robert's supervisor couldn't manage him or properly counsel him without the necessary knowledge of Robert's emotional intelligence.

While EQ problems and the lack of measuring them caused failure, knowledge of his emotional intelligence was the beginning of better performance and great success for Robert.

■ EQ Problems Can Ruin Personal Relationships

Sally was raised in an upper middle-class family by good parents. She had a high IQ and made good grades in high school. She had many friends and appeared to be well adjusted. At age twenty, she married a man she had dated at college. Rick also came from a good home, was attractive, possessed a very high IQ, and was doing well in school. For the first six years of marriage their relationship seemed to be ideal. Rick had a great job and made a high income. They lived in a beautiful house in a nice part of town.

However, by their twelfth year of marriage, Sally was clinically depressed and was abusing drugs. Rick stayed away from home as much as possible and also began to have an affair. He was having trouble doing his job and eventually quit. Sally and Rick's children, though they were all very intelligent, were having trouble in school—primarily behavioral problems. Sally quit her job and separated from her husband.

Every outward measurement would have predicted that Sally would lead a happy and well-adjusted life and that the couple would stay happily married. Yet, as you may have guessed by now, emotional intelligence was responsible for the downfall of Sally, Rick, their jobs, their marriage, and their children.

Sally grew up having low self-esteem. As a result, she needed much attention and praise. Although he was a responsible man, Sally's father had been very sparing with these rewards. In part, she was attracted to Rick because he initially was very positive about her. However, his attention and praise were only temporarily heightened because of the newness of the relationship and because it seemed to work in winning Sally's commitment to him.

As the honeymoon effect faded, Rick began to be more like he had been before meeting Sally. He became emotionally distant and focused more on his work. Sally responded to this distance by complaining about how much he worked, etc. Rick was not comfortable with conflict and withdrew from it, spending even less time with Sally, who in turn doubled her complaints. Rick, who basically had a negative attitude, began to focus on what he didn't like about Sally. Because he had a temper, at times he would explode with caustic criticism.

Sally was depressed by the blow to her self-esteem and by the general lack of reward in her life. She soon turned to drug abuse to block her negative feelings. The couple's arguments were very upsetting to the children, who then developed school problems and sleep disorders. At about this time, Rick became attracted to someone else who happened to meet his needs for attention. The extramarital affair that ensued caused further negativism in the marriage. As the conflict and emptiness in the marriage continued, both Sally and Rick found it progressively more difficult to work at their jobs.

■ A High EQ Builds Personal Relationships

By all rights, this marriage was dead and buried. Sally and Rick hated each other and were each emotionally destroyed. The children were hurting as a result, and their lives and their classrooms were disrupted. The companies that Sally and Rick worked for each suffered a loss.

Yet, somehow Sally was able to find help. One of her old friends, a counselor, had heard about her plight and set up a meeting with her. They began their counseling with the Simmons Personal Survey. The Survey quickly revealed the EQ problems that were causing Sally difficulty.

It was immediately apparent that Sally had low self-esteem and that she overemphasized the importance of her husband's opinions of her. Work was then begun to develop her self-esteem and to develop a rewarding focus that was not dependent upon her husband. She also needed a more positive outlook. Her view of her world had become totally negative. This same problem had earlier caused her to complain more to her husband. Because she was indecisive, she also needed directive counsel about even small matters like when to pay a bill.

As is often the case, Sally's spouse refused to participate in the counseling, although he did finally join the process several years later. Therefore, all of the initial reconstruction of the family had to be done through Sally. After just two to three meetings and within a few months, Sally was no longer depressed and no longer used drugs. She got a job, which she has now held for more than twenty years. After a few months of counseling, Sally and Rick reconciled. Their children's emotional states slowly returned to normal, and their school problems eventually cleared up.

While Sally's results were good, the healing process took time and hard work. She and Rick have had significant struggles throughout the years. Sally's marital recovery partially depended upon a spouse who would not get the same help she did. We tell her story as a reminder that miraculous total character overhauls like Robert's don't always occur. However, almost everyone can make very significant adjustments in their emotional intelligence with noticeable results occurring in a matter of weeks or a few months.

■ Defining Emotional Intelligence

Emotional intelligence is the emotional needs, drives, and true values of a person and guides all overt behavior. A person's interests tell you what a person likes to do. (Robert, for instance, liked the idea of being a manager.) A person's mental and physical skills tell you what a person can do. (Robert knew how to perform.) However, a person's emotional intelligence determines what they do and will do. (Robert's typical job performance was determined by his emotional intelligence.)

EQ largely determines your success in relating to people and your success in any given job. Characteristics such as responsibility, consideration for others, and sociability tend to build relationships. Other characteristics like selfishness, negativism, and hostility will mar any personal relationship.

A person can be very intelligent, have had good formal education for a job, have had years of experience in a job, be interested in the job, and still fail in the job because his or her emotional intelligence did not fit the job. For example, without assertiveness and social tendencies, a person cannot be an effective salesperson. Without the tendency to concentrate on detail and stay on task, a person will not excel as a chemist.

■ Other Success Factors

While emotional intelligence is the single most important factor in predicting relational and job success, other factors are also important and should always be evaluated. These other areas are: technical skills, specific knowledge, mental abilities, physical fitness, physical appearance, interest in a particular type of work, aspirations and career goals, and life circumstances that either support or hinder performance. Even with a super EQ, Robert would not have become a star performer if he had no restaurant training, was mentally disabled, had a bad heart, had a horrible personal appearance, really wanted to be a watchmaker, and had a marriage that was falling apart.

When you consider EQ, recognize that everyone has strengths as well as areas that get in their way. No one is perfect. Further, what is "best" or "ideal" will vary, depending on the demands of the environment. A quality that is not good for one environment (e.g., strong demandingness in a worker) can be quite good in another environment (e.g., strong demandingness in the president of an organization). Robert's original character prepared him to be an outstanding worker but not an outstanding manager.

■ Emotional Intelligence Varies in Degree

We have found that each area of emotional intelligence can be divided into one hundred significant increments or score levels. A person is not just decisive or indecisive. Very low scorers on this scale are dependent on guidance from others and avoid making decisions. Moderate scorers can make their own decisions but prefer advice and guidance. High scorers enjoy problem solving yet will share the decision-making process with others. Extremely high scorers are powerful decision makers who feel the need to control the outcomes of decisions.

In general, a low score represents a low amount of energy invested in that area of emotional intelligence. This person has little motivation here—this is a weak drive. She or he tends to fear and to avoid strong performance in the area. A low score on commitment to work means that the person avoids work. The person will do as little as he or she absolutely has to in order to meet his or her basic needs. A moderate to high score may be well balanced. The person has a strong motivation and drive. He or she confidently performs in this area, yet is free from avoidance and compulsion. A high scorer in commitment to work will work hard and stay on task while at the same time reserving time for rest, recreation, and relationships.

Extremely high scorers are highly motivated and driven in this specific area of emotional intelligence. They have much strength in the area. However, they are compulsive about their performance. They are tense about performing strongly in the area and (perhaps subconsciously) fear weak performance.

They are like a race car that has been built for extra performance. However, this excessive emphasis usually makes them lopsided in their priorities. A race car may go from zero to one hundred in ten seconds but get lousy gas mileage, make excessive noise, carry only one passenger, and not be allowed on the city streets. A person who has an excessive commitment to work may work seventy hours a week and be very appreciated by the boss. However, there may be a spouse and children at home who are not so pleased.

■ EQ Affects Compatibility

Compatibility with an environment, with a job, and with other people is heavily based upon one's level of emotional intelligence. For a person to be happy working alone at a remote oil pumping station in Alaska, a low level of sociability may be best. People with strong needs to be with other people have difficulty with isolation.

People who are opposites often are attracted to each other because they admire the opposite characteristic. Many quiet people have been drawn to those who are more friendly and outgoing. Many indecisive people enjoy being with others who are confident in making decisions.

However, over time, opposites generally develop conflicts. The quiet person may desire to stay at home and watch television, while the highly sociable person wants to be with new people in large gatherings. The pessimistic person may argue with the optimistic person about how bad a person, thing, or situation is.

Through insight into EQ, people who are naturally incompatible can come to appreciate those who are opposite them and work with them as a team. The reserved person can learn to appreciate how the social person can handle encounters such as birthdays, car pools, and relations with the neighbors, etc., for the family. The optimistic person can learn to appreciate how the pessimistic person can find problems that need to be fixed.

■ A Person's EQ Is Often Not Known

It's difficult to know a person's true emotional intelligence. Most people try to put their best foot forward for the public. In job interviewing, candidates play the "win-the-job game." The game usually involves the candidate dressing up better than normal and being ready to answer all of the interviewer's questions the way that interviewer would like them to be answered. In preparing, the candidate may have attended the "get-the-job-you-want" interviewing school. He or she also may have paid megadollars to the "we-make-you-look-famous" (even if you're not) resumé writing service. On the resumé, small tasks are often blown up to sound like major accomplishments.

In playing the game, interviewers are not allowed to ask candidates many questions that actually have to do with job performance. When interviewers call references, the rules clearly state that references are to tell the interviewers as little as possible and err on the positive side. Without the use of a tool like the Simmons Personal Survey that measures EQ, most interviewers and their companies lose the game about 50 percent of the time.

While putting up a false facade is very common in the hiring process, it also is a common occurrence in our personal lives. The "dating game" is very similar to the "win-the-job game." In the dating game, people try to look better than they usually do and try to do what the other person likes (even if it's not something they would normally want to do). They temporarily lose weight, take up new sports, and eat food they don't like, etc. Weeks and months may go by before the real person is seen.

About 50 percent of marriages end in divorce when spouses sadly find that they didn't marry the person they thought they were marrying. Within the first year of marriage, individual emotional intelligence problems and emotional intelligence incompatibilities begin to surface, and many couples don't know how to work through these problems.

Maintaining a facade is also at work on the dark side of our society. A very kindly eighty-year-old gentleman who lives in a quiet neighborhood with his elderly wife turns out to be a chronic and active pedophile. And every day conmen trick people out of their money.

Many people simply do not know themselves. Some people think they are loving when in fact they are very cold. Some think they are courageous but are really quite timid. In some cases, this lack of awareness is due to an ego defense mechanism designed to keep the person from feeling bad about himself or herself. In other cases, the person may have been given the wrong feedback from significant others, distorting self-perception. If a mother always praises a child's performance, even when it is poor, the child can feel very good based only upon the incorrect opinions of the parent. Lack of feedback from a variety of sources can cause a person to draw the wrong conclusions.

■ How Stable Is EQ?

There has long been an argument in the field of psychology about whether a person has a definite stable emotional intelligence trait (such as assertiveness) that determines how the person will behave. Trait theorists have argued that people do have stable characteristics. Trait theorists would say that a person who is assertive would be assertive most of the time. Behaviorists have argued that a person's behavior is situation specific. That is, a person may be assertive in one situation and not be assertive in another. Our research has shown that neither of these arguments is totally correct.

Emotional intelligence can be either static or changeable. Some people feel and behave very consistently. For example, they may feel nonassertive and act nonassertively in almost every circumstance they are in. While consistency reduces stress, too much consistency may not be adaptive in dealing with circumstances that vary. The consistently nonassertive person may need at times to be assertive in saying no to a salesperson or in returning a faulty product.

Other people have more variation in their emotional intelligence. They may feel compliant at times and at other times feel very assertive. They may be compliant with some people and with others be very assertive. Or they may consistently feel compliant, yet consistently be assertive. Some variation is healthy and adaptive, but too much variation involves large swings in feelings and behavior, resulting in much stress.

For most people, their basic emotional intelligence is apparent by the age of six and is still shifting during adolescence.

Once their emotional intelligence has been formed in adolescence, most people do not change it significantly, although conscious efforts to change emotional intelligence will result in emotional intelligence change—such as in the cases of Robert and Sally. While emotional intelligence tends to be rather consistent over time, some people are in the process of moving up or down in a given area of emotional intelligence. For example, some people are actively in the process of developing their assertiveness. Others who have been too bossy may have received helpful feedback from others and are trying to reduce their assertiveness.

■ Emotional Intelligence Is in the Brain

Emotional intelligence, like intellectual intelligence, is mostly a function of the brain. Emotional responses (how we feel about and value things), both innate and learned, are stored in the limbic system of the brain. A feeling or motivation that is purely emotional and nonverbal may reside in the limbic system alone. Decisions we have made about what is right and what is wrong, what we should and shouldn't do, what works and what doesn't work, are stored in the neocortex of the brain but have emotional values and connections found in the limbic system. Purely factual matters like where we live, what two plus two equals, and how to cook an egg are stored almost solely in the neocortex.

While emotional intelligence is stored in the brain, it involves and interacts with the total person—mental, physical, emotional, and behavioral. For example, when Robert was not assertive he may have perceived (with his eyes, retinal nerve, and visual cortex) that an employee was not working at his workstation. His memory (in the neocortex of the brain) tells him that based on his training, this is inappropriate. Emotionally (stemming from the limbic system in the brain), he feels angry, which tenses muscles, makes his heart pump faster, etc.

His neocortex reminds him that this situation calls for confronting the employee. This triggers a visual image of the employee disliking or disrespecting him, just as others have done in the past—making him feel worthless. This thought is connected to fear (which again comes from the limbic system of the brain). His face pales, his hands get cold, and his stomach has butterflies. He decides not to face this anxiety and so does not say anything to the employee.

■ How Emotional Intelligence Develops

How do we develop and become the way we are? Why does one person become assertive and another compliant? Why does one become a hard worker and another become lazy? Why does one become kind or friendly and another hostile? This occurs by the interaction of three main influences: heredity, learning, and physical or chemical changes in the body brought on by external forces. We typically think of these as nature, nurture, and injury.

Heredity or Nature

Each person inherits through the genetic process certain characteristics and tendencies from his or her biological parents. Some characteristics are totally determined. Others are only partially influenced. For instance, one's height potential, hair color, and eye color are totally determined. However, emotional intelligence traits such as hard work, hostility, friendliness, or courage are only partially influenced by one's genetic heritage.

The emotional intelligence of a child's parents is passed on to the child by chromosomes just as eye color is. Children are born with certain emotional intelligence tendencies. Some are more active, while others are passive. Some are irritable, while others are more patient. Some are quiet, while others are more assertive. Some children are naturally more cautious, while others explore more. Some seem to bond well with their parents, while others remain more aloof. Disorders like depression tend to run in families even when the children haven't been raised by their biological parents. These basic, innate emotional intelligence tendencies appear to reside in the limbic system. They are not caused by direct experience.

Robert, for instance, was born highly intelligent. To the best of our knowledge, he was also born with a tendency to be active, positive, passive, nurturing, and quiet.

Regardless of who our parents are, we all inherit the same basic human needs. In the 1970s, Abraham Maslow identified five basic human needs. The first one is biological in nature. Everyone has a need for food, water, etc. Second is the need for safety (i.e., the need to have a stable, structured, and predictable environment). Third, we all need to feel that we belong and are lovable. Fourth, all humans need to feel esteemed and respected. Finally, we have a need to reach our full potentials, capacities, and to exercise our talents. Psychologists often refer to this as the need for self-actualization.

These needs motivate us to develop our emotional intelligence. Emotional intelligence is developed as we find ways to cope with our environment to meet these basic needs.

Learning or Nurture

As mentioned above, we start out in life with our inherited qualities, predispositions, and basic human needs. From the day we are born, we are constantly striving to behave in ways that we believe will meet these needs.

Our beliefs and opinions about how to meet our needs are developed through our life experiences—what we see, hear, or learn about. We can learn from what happens to us— direct experience—or from what we have seen others do and what happened to them—vicarious experience. In this context, the environment of children includes their parents, siblings, neighbors, teachers, and acquaintances, as well as the physical environment—their home, neighborhood, television, or movies.

On the basis of these experiences, we draw conclusions about what we are like, what the world is like, and how to cope best with life's demands. We learn to like, say, and do what we believe will result in positive consequences for us. We also learn to dislike and avoid saying and doing what we believe will result in negative consequences.

When parents model achievement and reward it, their children tend to work hard and are usually goal-oriented. Children who are punished for emotional expression tend to inhibit this expression. Children of nurturing parents who reward nurturing behavior tend to become more nurturing as well. Children who have been neglected and not rewarded for social contact tend to have less motivation and are less social.

Another way to describe how we learn our emotional intelligence is that it involves making decisions. A child who is neglected or criticized will often decide that he or she is worthless. Children who are mistreated may decide that they have to take care of themselves since no one else will. As a result, they may decide not to trust and begin to look out only for number one. Someone who has been abused may decide to take vengeance. Children who have been physically or emotionally abused often act out with anger and hostility.

While emotional intelligence is often created with conscious awareness, it can be developed without any conscious thought. This involves a classical or stimulus-response relationship. A stimulus gains the ability to trigger a response that something else (another stimulus) already causes—because the first stimulus has been paired or associated with the second stimulus.

For example, physical pain is innately unpleasant. If a parent abuses a child by beating him or her, the parent can be associated with the pain and may be avoided. If a child's father cannot play with her because the father is always working, the child can develop a negative feeling about work itself. Because these feelings can be subconscious and are at the emotional level, the person may not be able to offer any explanation for his or her reaction.

Our emotional responses can be very general or more focused. If a person has had an emotional response to a particular event, he may respond in the same way to similar events. If a child has been rejected by his parents, he may develop a fear of rejection by all people. He may then begin to withdraw from all people. This is called generalization.

The effects of generalization are often limited by the process of discrimination, or learning to distinguish between similar events and to respond only to the appropriate one. For example, a child may learn through experience that his parents may reject him, but his grandmother and best friend won't. This child is likely to be open with his grandmother and friend but withdraw from his parents.

Sometimes it appears that people learn emotional responses by soaking them up from others. This is a subconscious process that appears to happen without conscious reasoning or thought. A child from a good family can become friends with a child from an abusive family. The abused child hates her parents and talks about them in a negative way. The child from the good family can develop negative feelings toward her parents just by being around the other abused child.

People who are not fearful of certain things can become fearful of them by being around someone who is terrified of something—even when the person developing the fear never had a direct negative experience with the feared object or situation. Monster stories told by one child can terrify another child. Stories about horrible storms can terrify someone who has never been in such a storm.

Positive feelings also can be soaked up by being around positive people. Some people can cheer others up just by their own personal happiness, cheerfulness, and positive outlook.

Physical and Chemical Influences or Injury

Sometimes what we are to become is altered by physical or chemical changes in the body. Brain damage, for instance, can have far-reaching effects such as loss of physical control of body parts, emotional intelligence changes, or loss of memory. A brain tumor or head injury often results in unexplained anger and hostility.

While many chemical abnormalities are hereditary, some are caused by what we do to our body. For instance, if a person takes certain drugs, he may hallucinate, be hyperactive, or be overly sedate. Withdrawal from certain drugs can cause these same kinds of symptoms because the body has come to depend on them.

■ Physical Consequences of Emotion

Strong emotion can be the cause of many physical disorders. Anxiety may cause stomach ulcers, twitches, shaking, cold feet and hands, or diarrhea. Anger can cause high blood pressure and tension headaches. There is even evidence to suggest that strong emotional crises damage the brain, causing further overreactions to many common occurrences.

■ Emotional Intelligence Traits and Types

In the following chapters, we will detail the twenty-six basic emotional intelligence types discovered in the Simmons Management Systems' research. These types represent what is measured at the lower and higher ends of the thirteen emotional intelligence scales we have developed. For each of the types, we will give a real-life example of a person who fits the type. We'll describe the feelings, attitudes, and behavior of this type. We'll discuss what can cause a person to be this way and offer solutions to any problems that person typically may have. We will also discuss how these types interact in personal relationships, and how you can predict the success or failure of relationships based on emotional intelligence.

As you read through this material, try to think of people you know who fit each type. Also try to determine which types fit you the best. The information shared will provide you with an opportunity to develop better ways of relating to people you know and to promote growth in your own emotional intelligence.

The basic emotional intelligence types we discuss are: The Slow-paced Person, The Fast-paced Person, The Relaxed Person, The Stressed Person, The Faultfinding Person, The Positive Person, The Humble Person, The Self-assured Person, The Leisurely Person, The Hardworking Person, The Spontaneous Person, The Careful Person, The Routine Person, The Change-oriented Person, The Cautious Person, The Courageous Person, The Hesitant Person, The Decisive Person, The Compliant Person, The Assertive Person, The Intolerant Person, The Tolerant Person, The Self-willed Person, The Considerate Person, The Reserved Person, and The Social Person.

Chapter 2

Measuring Emotional Energy

Emotional energy is the first of the thirteen areas of emotional intelligence that we will cover in this book. You already know about physical energy—the energy used for lifting things, walking, running, etc. Emotional energy, however, is the energy a person has to cope with stress, frustration, conflict, or pressure—that part of physical energy used to accomplish personal drives.

While physical energy and emotional energy are similar in degree for most people, in some people they can vary greatly. A person with high physical energy can have low emotional energy. In this case, the person may be able to run five miles but has not become emotionally mature. This person may not have a high EQ in areas such as commitment to work, decisiveness, consideration for others, or assertiveness.

A person with low physical energy will not have high emotional energy since physical energy is the basis for emotional energy. A person's ability to handle stress is definitely limited by physical energy.

Emotional energy is like a battery. If you have a lot of emotional energy, you can be very active and cope with much stress. With high emotional energy, you can invest yourself in many areas such as career, education, friends, hobbies, family, and household duties. If you have low emotional energy, you can still be successful by:

- Minimally investing yourself in a variety of areas.
- Focusing all of your energy in a few areas.
- Working to increase emotional energy.

■ Low Emotional Energy— the Slow-paced Person

Sam was a custodian for a small three-tenant office building. His job involved dusting the furniture, vacuuming the carpets, taking out the trash, changing lightbulbs, changing washers in the water faucets, and many other small tasks needed to keep tenants happy. He lived by himself in a small room of the building and had few responsibilities outside of his job. Because he normally only had a few tasks on his daily to-do list, he could work slowly and still get everything done. Sam's job also provided him with the opportunity to take many breaks during the day. When you watch Sam, you notice how slowly he moves. Sam has low emotional energy. Yet, he manages and conserves the small amount of energy he has so that he does not tire out.

Strengths

The slow-paced person generally conserves energy and tends to be unhurried. This person usually avoids facing and dealing with stressful or difficult situations and has a low degree of motivation. Simple observation will find slow-paced people moving slowly and taking their time. They may spend much time resting. They are not generally involved in many activities or in vigorous activities. Note that because the slow-paced person has these tendencies, they are more able to tolerate environments that involve low activity.

Potential Difficulties

The slow-paced person may be too complacent to achieve his or her full potential and to meet the demands of a fast-paced environment. He or she has trouble maintaining a fast pace and wears down quickly. Once tired, the slow-paced person may perform poorly at tasks and suffer in other emotional intelligence areas. Slow-paced people recover from high stress very slowly. They may avoid difficult people, or if they do deal with interpersonal problems, they become emotionally exhausted.

Alan was a slow-paced person who, unlike Sam, did not find an environment that was compatible with his low emotional energy.

Alan had always been low to moderate in emotional energy due to lack of nurturing from his parents. Alan's father was emotionally distant and usually critical of him. Alan felt like he could never win with his dad. His parents did not get along well, and each focused his or her energy on either Alan or his older brother. Alan's dad spent time with Alan's brother and made him into a superachiever. Alan's mother sided with Alan. However, she did not encourage him to try to achieve.

As a result of this type of family influence, Alan never did well in school despite the fact that he was as intelligent as his brother. After high school, he attended two years of college but performed marginally and quit. Alan then got a job selling office equipment. He did moderately well until he was rejected by a girl he intended to marry. The girl was fast-paced and expected more activity and achievement than Alan could muster.

While Alan had always been a little depressed, this rejection threw him into a deep depression. Suddenly, Alan couldn't handle the demands of his sales job. He was soon fired. Unfortunately, Alan kept trying to get hired in fast-paced sales jobs where he inevitably failed and got fired. He would have been better off either getting help with his energy level or selecting a job that involved less energy expenditure.

Causes of Being Slow-paced

Low emotional energy may stem from a lack of stimulation or encouragement in childhood during important developmental years. These deficiencies can retard the development of a normal degree of motivation. When a child is not attended to and nurtured, he or she tends to withdraw and become less involved in what is going on in the environment.

Low emotional energy can be a result of frustration from harsh circumstances and general withdrawal. When people of any age suffer an emotional loss such as losing a spouse, losing a job, being rejected by a significant other, or becoming crippled, they may respond to the loss by becoming depressed. When a person feels sad and sees things negatively, it usually decreases his or her level of activity.

Low emotional energy can be caused by low physical energy. When people are in poor physical health, they do not have the physical energy necessary to fulfill their drives and motivations. Low physical energy can make it very difficult to do things like work hard, be assertive, or make decisions.

Poor health can involve simply being out of shape, not eating right, exercising, or getting enough rest. Other chronic medical problems such as mononucleosis, low blood sugar, or cancer also cause fatigue and decrease activity.

In some cases, low emotional energy is socially learned. A person may have had models—parents, teachers, or others—who maintained low levels of activity. These models may have been out of shape, physically ill, depressed, etc. The slow-paced person may have "soaked up" the emotions and attitudes of these significant others, even though he or she never experienced firsthand the actual causes of the low energy.

■ High Emotional Energy—
the Fast-paced Person

Fred is a very successful business entrepreneur who has built a huge company from nothing. He had an idea, sold investors on it, worked out arrangements with the bank, and started production. He hired his executives and managers and developed relationships with raw material suppliers, designed production procedures, and found a way to sell his products.

Fred spends most of his time flying from city to city, meeting with his executives, investors, and suppliers. He is heavily involved in the planning of new locations and buildings. Fred works about seventy hours or more a week.

While the building of this giant company involved the use of many emotional intelligence traits such as decisiveness, commitment to work, courage, etc., using this emotional intelligence took a tremendous amount of emotional energy. Without high emotional energy, Fred's ambitions would have been little more than pipe dreams.

Strengths

The fast-paced person is generally active, energetic, motivated, and not passive or depressed. These people have enough energy to perform in demanding settings. They thrive on active, demanding daily activities. Fast-paced people tolerate high stress well and recover quickly.

You can watch the fast-paced person moving quickly. These people tend to spend a moderate amount of time resting and seem to need less rest than others. They may successfully juggle many activities or choose highly vigorous activities.

The fast-paced person desires an environment that involves much activity, a busy schedule, high-energy expenditure, high standards of performance, stimulation, challenging, demanding, or stressful situations, and pressure.

Potential Difficulties

In a slow or nondemanding environment, the fast-paced person may not feel challenged and will probably want to do more than the job allows.

Very fast-paced people may be more powerful than their managers are prepared to deal with. They can be difficult to control—

not necessarily because of a rebellious spirit but more due to the sheer strength of their drives. They can be impatient with low-energy people over the amount or speed of their activity.

Very fast-paced people are often driven, pressured, and hurried to accomplish or to achieve. This causes more stress. If they are not blessed with a virtually indestructible body, they will be more prone to develop stress-related problems such as high blood pressure or heart disease.

While Fred eventually became an outstanding entrepreneur, he had a hard time in elementary school and in high school. Because he was very fast-paced, he found it difficult to sit still in class. He appeared to be hyperactive. This caused him to disrupt the class and to get into trouble with the teachers. He did not want to stay on the narrow track his teachers tried to keep him on. He would ask other questions that were not exactly on the subject. Fred was happiest at recess or in gym class.

After graduating from high school, Fred found it difficult to assume worker roles in every job. It was always difficult for him to stay within the confining limits of his job description. His ideas about how things could be done better were seldom appreciated by his managers. Finally, someone noticed some leadership ability in Fred and put him into a management position. He was happier as a manager, but management wasn't quite right for him either.

Fred needed to be in control, to not be blocked, to be able to express himself. He realized that the only way he could have this degree of freedom was to get into business for himself and be his own boss. This decision ultimately led to his becoming a very successful entrepreneur.

Causes of Being Fast-paced

To some extent high emotional energy can be inborn and genetically determined. Fast-paced people tend to be healthy, and a certain degree of energy springs from this health.

Being fast-paced can result from much positive stimulation or encouragement during childhood during important developmental stages. High energy also can be a result of an environment where success was seen as being possible despite difficult circumstances or where success was expected and rewarded.

■ Recognizing Emotional Energy Levels

Ask a person to describe a day or perhaps a week. Don't tell him what you are looking for. Just keep him talking about what he does.

If he is slow-paced, you may hear about:
- Few activities.
- Low investment in activities.
- Not feeling well much of the time.
- Much time spent resting.
- Tiring under stress.

If he is fast-paced, you may hear about:
- Many activities.
- High investment in activities.
- Feeling well most of the time.
- Minimal time spent resting.
- Not tiring easily under stress.

Now be observant of physical behavior. Look and listen. In the slow-paced person you may notice:

- Slow movements.
- Slow rate of speech.
- A tired look.
- Limp facial muscles.
- Sleepy, tired, or sick appearance.

In the fast-paced person you may notice:

- Fast movements.
- Fast rate of speech.
- An energetic look.
- Firm facial muscles.
- Wide open eyes.

■ Solutions to Problems

How Emotional Energy Relates to the Job
....

Some jobs such as emergency medical technician or operating room nurse do tend to conflict with being slow-paced. However, in most cases, being slow-paced or fast-paced does not determine the type of job you should choose. Being slow-paced or fast-paced has more to do with determining the nature of the environment where you will thrive.

In other words, individual career titles such as mechanic, horticultural worker, or musician, do not have a built-in demand for a certain amount of energy. A mechanic working in a slow-paced, rural environment may not need to be fast-paced. A mechanic working as a part of a NASCAR racing team does need to be fast-paced. While most jobs in the United States call for more than low energy, there are many exceptions.

Use energy, therefore, as a way to compare a person's energy level to a specific job that requires a specific amount of energy. And consider the relationship between managers and workers as it relates to emotional energy. For instance, place the fast-paced person under a strong manager who has equal or more emotional energy.

Relationship Compatibility

Slow-paced people normally feel more comfortable around and have fewer conflicts with other slow-paced people. They tend to agree on the level of activity, the pace involved in completing a task, and other important factors.

Fast-paced people normally feel more comfortable around and have fewer conflicts with other fast-paced people. They also tend to agree on the level of activity and the pace involved in completing a task, etc.

In personal relationships, a slow-paced person may be very attracted to a fast-paced person out of respect for that person's stamina and activity. But there's a tendency over time for slow-paced and fast-paced people to develop certain conflicts. Slow-paced people may feel that the expectations and demands of the high-energy person are unreasonable. Fast-paced people may feel confined by the lower activity level of the slow-paced person. These conflicts are solvable if any of three things happen:

1) The slow-paced person can become more fast-paced, as described under modifying the slow-paced tendency, below.

2) The fast-paced person can become more slow-paced, as described under modifying the fast-paced tendency, below.

3) The two people can learn to appreciate the value of one being slow-paced and the other fast-paced. They can also respect and appreciate the other qualities in one another.

The couple may develop a plan where the slow-paced person is often allowed to be slow-paced, and the fast-paced person is often allowed to be fast-paced. They also may trade or compromise. The slow-paced person may schedule some fast-paced activities, such as going to a sporting event, while the fast-paced person schedules some slow-paced activities, such as playing cards.

Making the Slow-paced Person Comfortable

To relate to slow-paced people just as they are, to make them comfortable, and to reduce conflict:

- Give them plenty of time to rest, relax, and sleep.
- Provide a peaceful setting.
- Protect them from high stress.
- Let them have lower activity.
- Give them a relaxed schedule.
- Allow them to work at a slower pace.
- Give them plenty of time to complete tasks.
- Be emotionally supportive.

- Be easy to get along with.
- Do not put pressure on them.
- Be patient.
- Don't rush them.
- Be relaxed and tolerant.
- Don't be demanding about the quantity or speed of their performance.
- Don't be argumentative or oppositional.
- Allow them to avoid stressful situations or to handle stress a little at a time.
- Allow them to pace themselves to avoid wasting energy.
- Help them to focus their energy on priorities and avoid getting spread too thin with too many activities.
- Let others handle settings and situations for them that involve higher activity or stress.
- Put them in situations with other slow-paced people.

Making the Fast-paced Person Comfortable

For success with fast-paced people:
- Give them much activity and a busy schedule.
- Provide stimulating, challenging, demanding, or stressful situations.
- Let them proceed at a fast pace.
- Don't slow them down or block their goals any more than needed.
- Channel their energy instead of blocking it.
- Let other people handle situations that may not be as active.
- Put them in situations with other fast-paced people.

Modifying the Slow-paced Tendency

To be more compatible with others, slow-paced people need to understand the value of high-energy, fast-paced people, and what drives them. If low emotional energy is a result of having low physical energy, then slow-paced people can follow tips designed to improve general health, such as correcting medical problems, exercising, resting, and eating for energy.

If depression is involved, slow-paced people should seek treatment. If the depression is a reaction to a loss or a lack of reward, do what can be done to change the circumstances.

If low emotional energy is not physically based, it can be raised by increasing other emotional intelligence qualities, such as commitment to work or assertiveness, that are lower than ideal by following the solutions discussed in those chapters of this book.

Modifying the Fast-paced Tendency

If you're fast-paced, decreasing the pace or level of activity is usually not necessary, unless you are developing a stress-related problem such as high blood pressure, heart disease, an ulcer, or a general vulnerability to disease. High emotional energy can be adjusted by decreasing other emotional intelligence qualities, such as commitment to work or assertiveness, that are higher than ideal. This can be accomplished by following the recommendations listed in following chapters.

To be more compatible with others, high-energy people should develop an awareness of the value of the contributions made by low-energy people, an understanding of the causes of low energy, and an awareness of the value of relaxation.

If a person is excessively active, has poor concentration, and is very impulsive in speech or in action, it's possible that he or she is hyperactive. This disorder is largely treatable with medication.

Managing the Slow-paced Person

Emphasize, model, require, and reward speed, activity, and quantity of work. With some people, discipline imposed for lack of speed, lack of activity, and lower quantity of work is highly successful.

Managing the Fast-paced Person

Emphasize, model, require, and reward staying within job limits or within relational agreements. In some instances discipline imposed for not staying within limits is needed. These people need a very strong manager to direct them.

■ Get Your Pencil—Checkup Time

To Make This Information Useful to You, You Must Apply It!

1) Write down the type of person you fit best (slow-paced or fast-paced).
2) Write down how being this way has helped and any specific problems it has caused.
3) If you have had problems with this area of emotional intelligence, then write down which solutions you will use to improve. Perhaps receive a desired reward for completing steps of your plan and for total completion.
4) Carry out the solutions you choose. Trying to change and repetition will make the action part of your character.

To Improve Relationships or to Help Others

1) Write down the type of person that someone you know fits best.
2) Write down how being this way has helped and any specific problems it has caused.
3) If this person has had problems with this area of emotional intelligence, then write down which solutions you will use to reduce conflict with that person or to build his or her performance. Perhaps this person can receive a desired reward for completing steps of the plan and for total completion.
4) If you feel that the person is able and willing to receive this feedback, share your new insight with that person and tell him or her about what you think needs to be done.

Chapter 3

Measuring Emotional Stress

E motional stress is the degree to which a person is troubled by uncomfortable feelings. These troubled feelings, whether or not we are consciously aware of them, place a degree of tension on the body and, in high amounts, disturb our physical performance.

Emotional stress is not a singular emotional intelligence trait. Instead, it is a summary of all of the factors (both environmental and personal) that are presently troubling or bothering a person.

■ Low Stress—the Relaxed Person

Ray is the owner and operator of a small service station located in a rural area quite a distance from the main highway. On an average day, he serves between ten and twenty customers. At least half of his customers are people he has known for years.

Ray is in no hurry to get to work each day. If he's twenty minutes late, he's not bothered, and no one usually knows. Free from the "rat race" that business people in larger cities often experience, he has no daily project planner. He doesn't even wear a watch. Ray has all he needs to be happy, has no financial worries, and is not pressured to get rich.

Even though his station is old and needs some repairs, Ray is satisfied with it. He's genuinely content with himself and with his circumstances, which is obvious in the cheerful disposition he shows to customers who drop in.

Ray works slowly or intermittently throughout the day. There's enough variety and challenge in his work to interest him. He pumps gas, fixes tires, changes oil, puts in batteries, and sells a few items (like drinks and chips) in his small store. He doesn't venture into fixing a motor, a transmission, or any other difficult mechanical repair, regarding those projects as too much of a hassle. He usually stays comfortable inside the air-conditioned sales area, sitting in a chair, drinking a soft drink.

Day after day, Ray makes just enough decisions to feel in control, such as when to come in, when to leave, or what brand of chips to sell. Ray is just assertive enough to get customers to pay for their gas, for his service, or for the products he sells.

When not at the service station, Ray goes fishing or shoots pool with his friends at the diner next door. He has nearly total inner-peace. Ray is doing just what he wants to do in life and feels no pressure to do anything else.

Note that Ray was not avoiding work, people, or making decisions. If he did, he would feel stress since any avoidance involves fear or anxiety. Negative situations that drive a person to avoid them also cause stress. Ironically, people who board themselves up inside a room and do nothing are actually quite stressed. Withdrawn people are often fearful and suffering.

Strengths

The relaxed person is calm, untroubled, unworried, and unpressured. He or she is not fearful, avoiding, pressured, or compulsive. These folks don't try to do any more than they feel like doing. Nor do they try to act differently than they really feel. They lead a truly happy and peaceful life and don't have enough stress to disturb performance or cause physical symptoms.

The characteristics of truly calm and relaxed people are fairly predictable. They tend to have a moderately active lifestyle, a positive attitude, and good self-esteem. They are neither sloppy nor worried about doing things perfectly. They neither avoid work nor pressure themselves to work. They are not confined by compulsive routines or compelled to make constant changes. They are not fearful of physical discomfort, nor do they feel compelled to take large risks to prove themselves.

They feel comfortable making decisions but don't have to be in control of all decisions made. They are not afraid to express their opinions. Nor do they feel they always have to get others to do things their way. They are not quick to anger. Nor do they hold in their anger. They generally try to achieve win-win relationships, not "I win-you-lose" or " I lose-you-win" relationships. They can socialize but don't set out to win a popularity contest.

Potential Difficulties

As nice and ideal as being totally calm may seem, there is a downside. The main difficulty with calm people is that they are too complacent to truly reach their potential. They don't push themselves to deal with stressful situations. There are many things they could learn that they do not learn. Many problems could be solved that they do not solve. They don't do things as well and as precisely as many would like. There are people they could help that are not helped. They use a smaller percentage of their brain than do more achieving people. They may never fully use their muscles and may "sit on" their talents without developing them.

These people are in the middle of the road. They don't fit the more demanding environments that most employers expect. In general they run the course of least resistance. Their motto in life isn't "do it," it's "take it easy."

Why Some People Are So Relaxed

When the relaxed person was growing up, chances are that he or she was in an environment with little emphasis on achieving in general. Working hard, striving for excellence, or taking leadership roles may not have been modeled, required, or rewarded. And yet, the environment was also not full of fear or anxiety.

While many communities may work to instill these values, more typically the relaxed person would come from slow-paced, rural areas rather than big cities or industrial environments.

In some cases, people get tired of a stressful job or environment and realize that they don't want to spend their life rushing to work, fighting rush-hour traffic, dealing with a negative boss, or talking to frustrating customers. These people may then choose a quieter, more peaceful job or setting and become more relaxed.

Lack of stress can, to some degree, be a result of peaceful, nearly ideal life circumstances. There may be money in the bank, food on the table, and a loving family that help a person overcome other stressful factors. There may be an absence of present circumstances that are harsh, such as a messy divorce, being fired, or going through a period of unemployment while bills stack up.

Stress is lower when a person's emotional intelligence matches his work or when it is compatible with someone he relates to. For example, a sociable, friendly person will be comfortable if he can work around others and chat a little. A quiet, reserved person will be comfortable if he can have some privacy from others.

While environmental circumstances can be very harsh, our feelings of stress can often be reduced or removed by choosing to think positively about a situation and by taking constructive action. People who have learned these attitudes have less stress.

■ Moderate Stress

The normally stressed person is reasonably calm and relaxed but is usually willing to do what is necessary to recognize, cope with, or to overcome stressful situations. These people have some stress in coping with life's challenges but not enough to disturb concentration, coordination, or physical performance.

They may be either more achieving than the calm person, or they may simply be more concerned about what is going on in their life. This moderate degree of stress is not harmful and can be beneficial—just enough stress to push a person toward his or her full potential.

■ High Stress—the Stressed Person

Strengths
··

The stressed person is strongly concerned about performance and about how to cope best in his or her environment. Stressed people are very concerned about what is going on in their lives. They may be either much more achieving than the calm person, or they may simply be much more concerned about what is going on in life.

Potential Difficulties
··

Stressed people are tense, troubled, worried, restless, or pressured. However, note that there are many different ways that people may be stressed. They are either fearful and avoiding or pressured and compulsive. They may try to do much more than they feel like doing. To please others or to cope with circumstances, they may try to act in ways they really don't feel comfortable acting. Their happiness and sense of peace is marred by stress over and over again.

They tend to extremes: either a very inactive lifestyle due to depression or a very active busy lifestyle; a negative, gloomy attitude or a denial of environmental problems; a low self-esteem or an excessively high opinion of self. They are either sloppy or worried about doing things perfectly. They either avoid work or pressure themselves to work. They are confined by compulsive routines or compelled to make constant changes. They are fearful of physical discomfort or feel compelled to take large risks to prove themselves.

They either feel uncomfortable making decisions or are compelled to be in control of all decisions made. They may be afraid to express their opinions or feel they always have to get others to follow them. They are either angry, or they hold in their anger. They generally try to achieve "I win-you-lose" or " I-lose-you-win" relationships, not win-win relationships. They either are afraid to socialize or are striving to win a popularity contest.

Being at either end of any of the emotional intelligence scales can be stressful. The very low end usually involves fear, anxiety, and avoidance of performance. The very high end usually involves pressure, tension, and compulsion to perform.

Physical Results of Stress

The stressed person has enough stress to be at risk for stress-related problems, including headaches, lower concentration, decreased coordination, muscular tension, upset stomach, hampered work performance, susceptibility to illness, high blood pressure, heart failure, and excessive tiredness. They may have difficulties getting to sleep, staying asleep, and feeling rested, and are at risk for substance abuse and eating disorders.

People with high emotional energy, as described in chapter 2, often can keep performing despite their stress. They may have a stomach ulcer but chew their Maalox and keep going. They also may pop aspirins for their tension headaches. Many people with high emotional energy can have a mass of troubling emotions playing inside of them but have enough energy to control these emotions and do their work, too.

Whether serious health problems result from stress depends to a large degree on how healthy the person is before the stress goes to work. Health is mostly determined by genetics but also includes the practice of good health habits such as proper diet and exercise.

Burl is vice president of sales for a rather small but fast-paced company that sells medical equipment to hospitals and doctor's offices. His average workload is ten hours a day, seventy hours a week. He is expected to sell, manage two other salespeople, and manage the office, which employs various clerical people. Burl is successful, and the president is pleased with his performance.

However, Burl is under tremendous stress that is actually killing him. He has tension headaches, an irritable stomach, recurring skin rashes, high blood pressure, and doesn't sleep well at night. In order to please his boss, he has to work long hours, but this creates problems at home with his wife and children who also want his time. His cellular phone is constantly ringing and exposing him to even more things to do in between the things he is already doing. His day is tightly scheduled. He is frequently checking his watch to make sure that he stays on schedule. Because he performs well, his boss piles more and more work on him.

Burl constantly worries about the adequacy of his performance. He feels inadequate but tries to act like everything is fine. He feels indecisive and nonassertive but constantly role-plays as being decisive and assertive. He is far out of his comfort zone.

Causes of Stress

There are many different ways to be stressed and, therefore, many different causes. Some of these will be discussed chapter by chapter as we address particular emotional intelligence factors. Look for either very low or very high emotional intelligence measures—very low optimism, very low self-esteem, excessive self-esteem, avoidance of work, or compulsion to work, for example.

Stress also can come from a reaction to present circumstances that are harsh. A person may be going through a messy divorce. His house may have just burned down. He may be unemployed, broke, and in debt.

Stress can be brought on when a person's emotional intelligence doesn't match her work or when it is incompatible with someone she relates to. For example, a sociable, friendly person will be stressed if she must work in isolation from others. A quiet, reserved person will be stressed if she is responsible for meeting and greeting new people.

In both pleasant and unpleasant circumstances, our feelings of stress are often increased by choosing to think negatively about a situation. Stress also can be increased by not taking appropriate action—either by avoiding a situation and letting problems develop or by deciding to take on more than we can really do.

■ Solutions to Problems

Stress and Jobs

In most cases, being relaxed or stressed does not determine the type of job a person should choose but has more to do with determining the nature of the environment that works best for someone. A relaxed person will want a relaxed environment. A very stressed person probably should not be placed into a very stressful setting due to the potential for emotional, performance, and physical problems.

Stress and Relationships
....

Relaxed people are typically most comfortable with other relaxed people and probably will not feel comfortable around highly stressed people.

Making the Relaxed Person Comfortable
....

To relate best to relaxed people:
- Give them plenty of time to rest, relax, and sleep.
- Provide a peaceful setting.
- Let them have lower levels of activity.
- Give them a relaxed schedule.
- Allow them to work at a slower pace.
- Give them plenty of time to complete tasks.
- Be easy to get along with.
- Don't put pressure on them.
- Be patient. Don't rush them.
- Be relaxed and tolerant.
- Don't be demanding about the quantity or speed of their performance.
- Don't be argumentative or oppositional.
- Allow them to avoid stressful situations or to handle stress a little at a time.
- Let other people handle settings and situations with them or for them that involve higher activity or stress.
- Put them around other relaxed people.

Making the Stressed Person Comfortable

To best relate to stressed people:
- Don't do things that will increase their stress level.
- Find out exactly what stresses them (whether inside the job or outside), and help them avoid it or solve the problem.

Modifying the Relaxed Tendency

- Increase commitment in areas of emotional intelligence where you are low, such as commitment to work, attention to detail, and assertiveness, following the suggested solutions chapter-by-chapter.
- Be more willing to experience the anxiety involved in stretching to meet environmental demands.

Modifying the Stressed Tendency

- Adjust stress by either working to increase very low areas of emotional intelligence or to decrease very high areas.
- Work out solutions to environmental situations presently causing stress.
- Think positively about situations and take constructive action.
- Work out emotional intelligence incompatibilities in your job or in your relationships.
- Get seven to eight hours of sleep each night, regular aerobic exercise, and eat a well-balanced diet.
- Learn ways to relax. Imagine and totally focus on a pleasant scene. Do slow, deep breathing. Momentarily tense a muscle and then let it go. Do this for each muscle group.

- Seek more relaxed settings, people who are easier to get along with, or a job that is less stressful.
- If nothing seems to help, consider seeing a doctor who may prescribe medication to help you relax.

Get Your Pencil—Checkup Time

To Make This Information Useful to You, You Must Apply It!

1) Write down the type of person you fit best (relaxed or stressed).
2) Write down how being this way has helped and any specific problems it has caused.
3) If you have had problems with this area of emotional intelligence, then write down which solutions you will use to improve. Perhaps receive a desired reward for completing steps of your plan and for total completion.
4) Carry out the solutions you choose. Trying to change and repetition will make the action part of your character.

To Improve Relationships or to Help Others

1) Write down the type of person that someone you know fits best.
2) Write down how being this way has helped and any specific problems it has caused.
3) If that person has had problems with this area of emotional intelligence, then write down which solutions you will use to reduce conflict with him or her or to build that person's performance. Perhaps he or she can receive a desired reward for completing steps of the plan and for total completion.
4) If you feel that the person is able and willing to receive this feedback, share your new insight with that person and tell him or her about what you think needs to be done.

Chapter 4

Measuring Optimism

Measuring optimism tells you to what degree you see your world in a positive or negative light. In this chapter, we'll discuss the extremes—the faultfinding person and the positive person—and the strengths and potential problems associated with each of them.

■ Low Optimism—the Faultfinding Person

Fran works as an IRS auditor. Her job is to examine the financial records of taxpayers to find where they've been inaccurate or fraudulent. She doesn't waste her time evaluating what each person has done right. In her mind, that's not her job. Instead, she has a knack for getting right to the problem.

Through years of experience, Fran knows that many people are unable to figure their taxes correctly and that others try to cheat Uncle Sam. She has become wary of people's attempts to conceal income and to overestimate expenses.

Like Fran, Frank, who is a policeman, feels that he has to be wary of others. He must be watching for ways that others break the law, whether they're speeding, driving recklessly, committing robbery, or dealing drugs. When he sees an offense, he must apprehend the person and point out what he or she did wrong. While writing a ticket for a violation, he must keep an eye on the person to make sure the person doesn't pull out a gun or a knife. Being wary is part of self-preservation in his job.

Strengths

The faultfinding person, who measures low on optimism, is quickly and naturally able to see what is wrong with things or people. Faultfinders have a keen ability to spot errors and problems. They can often suspect what is wrong with something before it occurs.

Faultfinders aren't easily tricked by others. Their awareness of potential risk or danger allows them to avoid problems or to try to solve them early on. Faultfinders thrive in an environment that involves finding risks, errors, problems, or faults that need to be solved. They do best when they don't have to identify and communicate what is positive or good and where they do not have to encourage others. Their distrust of others can be very practical when they are around people who are likely to be untrustworthy.

Potential Difficulties

Faultfinders are inwardly rather serious, sober, fearful, and unhappy. Their view of reality is negatively biased, and they are often spending negative energy worrying about something.

Faultfinders may fail to see the good that exists and see things as being worse than they really are. They may upset, discourage, or depress others. Others who are around them may feel that no matter how hard they try, they are not perceived as doing something well enough or being good enough. Faultfinders can make other people feel unappreciated.

It's easy to recognize the faultfinders. They don't often smile and appear either serious or sad. When faced with a problem, they usually try to find who or what was at fault. They may say little that is positive about others' efforts or accomplishments.

If the faultfinding person is also assertive, you'll often find that person criticizing other people, things, or situations. He spends his time talking about what is wrong with a person, thing, or situation. He may mention distrust of the motives of others.

The faultfinding person doesn't work well in environments where others need encouragement or praise. Ideally, these people should not work with those who are easily depressed or offended. In an environment where others are very able and trustworthy, the faultfinding person's tendencies may cause unnecessary offense.

Mandy was excessively faultfinding. Add to her negative attitude a generous dose of assertiveness and anger, and the effects are even worse. Mandy criticized her husband until he couldn't take it anymore and left her. As a salesperson, she constantly pointed out to her sales manager how she did not like the limitations of her territory, her rate of commission, even her expense account. Mandy was always complaining about something. When the customer would complain about slow delivery, the wrong product being delivered, or about damaged merchandise, Mandy was quick to blame the company. She was so hard to take that when she came to town to visit the home office, her boss would resort to a few drinks to calm himself. Mandy eventually was fired for creating problems at work and for offending some important customers.

Causes of Low Optimism

Low optimism can be an innate part of personality present from birth. Some children are more irritable, harder to please, and don't appear to be naturally happy. Some of these children are bothered by medical problems, while others just don't have a sunny disposition.

Negativism can also develop in an environment where others talk about people, places, and things in a faultfinding manner, and where negative statements are socially rewarded with attention from others. The faultfinding person also may have experienced harsh circumstances. Hard times in the past can make you believe that focusing on problems is simply realistic. People who think it is a "dog-eat-dog" world may have suffered under the influence of people who acted selfishly and inconsiderately.

High Optimism—the Positive Person

Paul is a family counselor. He has the ability to see the good in his clients and to bring it out. His smile and cheerful disposition make his clients feel comfortable. He has faith that each person can be successful in life if they are shown the way. Paul's clients learn to believe in themselves and develop a positive attitude about others.

Paul praises good behavior, which helps to build appropriate habits and values. While Paul only makes a moderate income to support his family of five, he is positive about the counseling center and is thankful to have his position.

Strengths

Positive people are high on the optimism scale, tending to see the good in people, things, and situations. These positive thinkers are not generally critical of other people, things, or situations. They stay aware of the good things that others do, of their positive qualities, and of their potential. They tend to be trusting of others and of their motives.

If they also are assertive, you'll find them often praising others and giving compliments. They may mention trust when describing the motives of others. If they are also assertive, they may spend time talking about what is good about a person, thing, or situation.

When they look into the past, positive people see the good that happened. When they view present situations, they see the benefits and positive features. Even when thinking about negative situations, they can usually see the bright side. They are very optimistic and hopeful, believing that things will work out well. Because of this positive outlook on life, they are enthusiastic, excited, cheerful, and happy. These people tend to smile and look happy.

Psychological research has shown that a positive attitude is associated with handling stress better, having less stress-related problems, and with living longer.

The positive person prefers an environment that involves identifying and communicating what is positive or good, encouraging others, and where there is little to realistically worry about. The positive person does not want to focus totally on finding risks, errors, problems, or faults that need to be solved.

Compatible people are cheerful, trusting, happy, very positive, and optimistic. Positive people do well around people who need encouragement or appreciation and who are trustworthy, responsible, and able. They do best when they are around people who are not constantly faultfinding, distrustful, pessimistic, fearful, or skeptical.

Potential Difficulties

Very positive people may overlook or deny risk, situational problems, and faults. They may not see others' limitations or their inappropriate motivations and can end up being hurt by others. They may try hard to believe things are fine even when they're not—which may delay actual problem solving. Their view of reality is positively biased.

In an environment where there are many problems or risks, the very positive person may fail to see problems that exist or not fully evaluate them. They may see things as being better than they really are or see people as being better than they really are. Therefore, some problems may not be avoided or corrected. The behavior of people they trust may not measure up to what they were expected to do.

Ned was the owner and operator of a small business. His attitude was so positive that he didn't see the problems around him. He believed "everything would work out." However, everything was not working out. His customers frequently complained about poor quality service. Work done by employees had to be done over—sometimes several times—at the expense of the business. The business had developed a reputation in town for poor work. In addition, the company was in serious debt.

Ned's wife, in response to the job pressures, was seriously depressed, had high blood pressure, and was at risk for having a heart attack. She had a very negative attitude about what was going on. While many of her worries were realistic, some were excessive. The couple had many arguments about how well the employees did and about the chances of the business succeeding.

Despite all of this, Ned kept believing that everything was all right and that all would work out in the end. Ned soon lost his business and had to take a worker-level job for a competitor.

Causes of High Optimism

A highly positive attitude may have developed in an environment where others talked about people, places, and things in a positive and optimistic manner. During developmental years, significant others were probably not highly critical or pessimistic. However, regardless of the early developmental environment, a positive attitude may have been developed through receiving instruction or training on positive thinking.

The positive person may have had relatively few hard times in the past and may see a positive outlook as being realistic. However, very high optimism may be an ego defense mechanism against feeling fearful or depressed.

■ Identifying Optimism

Ask a person to describe her past jobs, bosses, coworkers, etc. Don't tell her what you are looking for. Just keep her talking about what happened and about how she felt.

If she is faultfinding, you may hear her:

- Criticize those around her or the job setting in general.
- Tell you about dangers, errors, problems, or faults.
- Talk about what she didn't like.

If she is positive, you may hear her:

- Being positive about those around her or the job setting.
- Tell you about what she liked.
- Talk about what was good about a person, thing, or situation.

You can learn a lot from observation. In the faultfinding person you may notice:

- Either a sad or very serious expression.
- Rare smiles.
- An expressionless or frowning face.
- Deep sighs.

In the positive person you may notice:

- A cheerful or happy expression.
- Frequent smiles.
- An easy laugh.

Other people, if asked, will probably be able to easily tell you about these types of characteristics.

■ Solutions to Problems

Optimism and Jobs
....

It is generally best to have a moderate to high amount of optimism for most circumstances and for most jobs. Strong negativism can hamper most relationships. Being carefree and naive can lead to danger.

If the job involves working with people who may be harmful, the degree of optimism should be moderate. This would apply to police work, being an auditor, or being a business consultant—especially a turnaround expert. If the job involves being encouraging and optimistic, especially in the face of adversity, optimism should be above average to high. This would apply to jobs such as a psychologist, marriage counselor, or special education teacher. The person who is carefree and naive should ideally be in an environment where people are trustworthy and where there are few potential or everyday dangers.

Optimism and Relationships
....

Faultfinding people normally feel more comfortable around and have fewer conflicts with other faultfinding people. Faultfinding people tend to agree on how bad a person, place, or thing was, is, or will be. However, faultfinding people will get on each other's nerves when their criticism is directed at one another instead of at the environment.

Positive people normally feel more comfortable around and have fewer conflicts with other positive people. They tend to agree on how good a person, place, or thing was, is, or will be. When positive people are positive about each other, it is usually enjoyed.

While a faultfinding person may be very attracted to a positive person because the positive person adds sunlight and cheer to an otherwise gray picture, there is a tendency over time for faultfinding and positive people to develop conflicts.

Faultfinders may disagree with highly optimistic people about how bad something was, is, or will be. The faultfinder will see the glass as being half empty while the optimist sees it as being half full. If optimism is extremely high, the very positive person may become irritated when others with less optimism attempt to discuss harsh realities. These conflicts are solvable if any of three things happen:

1) The faultfinding person can become more positive.

2) The positive person can become less optimistic.

3) The two people can learn to appreciate the value of one being faultfinding and the other positive. They can also respect and appreciate different qualities the other person has.

Making the Faultfinding Person Comfortable

To best relate to faultfinding people without changing them:

- Let them talk about risks, errors, problems, or faults that need to be solved.
- Show an interest in and a respect for their opinions about what is wrong.
- Let them know that you understand how they feel and why they feel that way.

- If their opinions are at all realistic, show your agreement with their ideas.
- Point out some things you dislike similar to what they dislike.
- Do not make them identify or communicate what is positive or good.
- Get others to handle situations where being positive is important.
- Put them around other faultfinding people, but watch out for people who might be negative about them.

Making the Positive Person Comfortable

To best relate to positive people without trying to change them:
- Let them identify and communicate what is positive or good or encourage others.
- Show an interest in and a respect for their positive opinions.
- Let them know that you understand how they feel and why they feel that way.
- If their opinions are at all realistic, show your agreement with their ideas.
- Point out some things you like that are similar to what they like.
- Do not make them focus on finding risks, errors, problems, or faults that need to be solved.
- Get others to handle situations where being faultfinding or critical is important.
- Put them around other positive people.

Modifying the Faultfinding Tendency

A friend or counselor could:

1) Listen to the person's opinion about what he or she thinks is wrong.
2) Restate what the faultfinding person said so he or she will know the helper understands.
3) Be respectful of that person's opinion.
4) As much as he or she is willing, get him or her to consider the positive side.

Self-help for the Faultfinding Person

- Learn to appreciate the value, feelings, and contributions of people with high optimism.
- Look for fewer faults and more good. A helpful sentence to keep in mind would be: "What is good or right about ____?"
- Keep a "positive" log. Every day write down ten or more positive things about circumstances, people, or things.
- Improve any life situation that may be causing pessimism. If the faultfinding nature is a reaction to negative environmental circumstances, then improving or correcting these situations can lead to a more positive outlook.
- Make the environmental influence more cheerful and positive. This includes the people you are with, what you read, what you see, what you listen to, etc.
- Be more thankful and positive. Smile more. Offer more praise or appreciation to others. Demonstrate confidence and trust in others.

Modifying the Positive Tendency

A friend or counselor could:
1) Listen to the person's opinion about what he or she thinks is good.
2) Restate what the positive person said so he or she will know the helper understands.
3) Be respectful of that person's opinion.
4) As much as he or she is willing, get him or her to consider potential problems, faults, and danger. Others may remind them of risk, problems, and faults.

Self-help for the Positive Person

- Learn to appreciate the value of people who are less positive and more faultfinding.
- Identify more of the negative/wrong in things, people, and situations. Ask the question:
  "What is negative or wrong about ____?"
- If the positive attitude is to the point of being unrealistic, keep a "negative" log. Every day write ten or more problems found in circumstances, people, or things.
- Face and correct more problems.
- Learn how to diplomatically criticize others' performance.

Managing the Faultfinding Person

Emphasize, model, require, and reward positive statements. Consider discipline for lack of positive statements or for negative statements.

Managing the Positive Person

Emphasize, model, require, and reward finding problems and telling others about them. Consider discipline for lack of faultfinding or constructive criticism.

Get Your Pencil—Checkup Time

To Make This Information Useful to You, You Must Apply It!

1) Write down the type of person you fit best (faultfinding or positive).
2) Write down how being this way has helped and any specific problems it has caused.
3) If you have had problems with this area of emotional intelligence, then write down which solutions you will use to improve. Perhaps receive a desired reward for completing steps of your plan and for total completion.
4) Carry out the solutions you choose. Trying to change and repetition will make the action part of your character.

To Improve Relationships or to Help Others

1) Write down the type of person that someone you know fits best.
2) Write down how being this way has helped and any specific problems it has caused.
3) If that person has had problems with this area of emotional intelligence, then write down which solutions you will use to reduce conflict with him or her or to build that person's performance. Perhaps he or she can receive a desired reward for completing steps of the plan and for total completion.
4) If you feel that the person is able and willing to receive this feedback, share your new insight with that person and tell him or her about what you think needs to be done.

Chapter 5

Measuring
Self-esteem

S elf-esteem is the tendency to value oneself and to be self-accepting. It measures how well people like themselves and how positively people see themselves.

Appropriate self-esteem is found in a minority of people in our society. Most people grow up without the proper degree of parental love and affection, usually resulting in low or conditional self-esteem but sometimes in a false overestimation of self-worth.

■ Low Self-esteem—the Very Humble Person

Helen is a general secretary for a small office. She's down-to-earth and never acts as if she's better-off than others. Helen is willing to hear from others about what she needs to do to improve, as long as the suggestions are accompanied by respect. When told to keep her work area neat, she sincerely apologized and said she would try to keep it better organized. When she had come in late a few times and was confronted about it, she apologized and started coming in on time. While she actually had some good reasons for being late, she didn't make excuses or blame other circumstances. Helen is accepting of others. Others feel that they have nothing to prove to Helen and that they can be themselves with her. She is very attractive but not vane.

Strengths

The humble person is very aware of what he or she perceives to be personal faults and shortcomings. The humble person believes there is room for improvement and is not grandiose about his or her personal qualities.

Humility should be distinguished from low self-confidence. A person who lacks self-confidence believes that he or she is incapable of achieving or accomplishing difficult tasks, such as building a company, or of overcoming adversity, such as stiff competition.

In contrast, the person with a low self-esteem score either has a low sense of self-worth—"I am no good."—or, just as likely, a conditional sense of self-worth—"I am only a good person if I achieve or please other people."

If humble people also have positive attitudes and are sociable, they may be open with others about their perceived faults. Otherwise, humble people may be very private about their perceived faults.

Potential Difficulties

Very humble people are offended or hurt easily by criticism and rejection. Because they expect criticism and rejection from others, humble people often perceive it when none was intended. This can cause them to be offended, hurt, and angry and to respond in defensive ways despite the explanations of others to the contrary.

They may avoid pursuing relationships with people they feel are better than they are and settle for people they regard as being at their level—even if the relationship is unsatisfactory in many ways. To avoid the rejection they believe will come, they may prematurely reject others.

It is often hard for very humble people to believe that others truly like or care about them or that others mean the positive things that they say to them. If humble people maintain a relationship with someone they view as being highly desirable, they may be troubled with doubts of whether that person can really choose them over others.

Very humble people find it difficult to believe that they can make the personal change to their emotional intelligence necessary to improve themselves. This makes them uncomfortable with and inflexible about change. The very humble person is typically angered or demotivated by criticism, abuse, neglect, and rejection. People who are proud, highly self-accepting, or who look down on others can exacerbate the humble person's low self-esteem.

While Helen was modest and willing to accept her mistakes, she suffered from very low self-esteem. She didn't seem to know how able and attractive she truly was. It was as if she saw something different in the mirror than what others saw when they looked at her. Helen would constantly put herself down. When she made a mistake, she would say things like "That was really stupid!"

Helen was involved in a codependent relationship with a man who was not good for her. He would regularly get drunk and beat her mercilessly. He was also very critical of her. Instead of leaving, Helen would wear makeup and long sleeves to hide the bruises. She continued to tolerate the abuse because she believed she deserved it. She had previously been married to a man who was also emotionally abusive of her but did finally divorce him. Finally, Helen had to quit her, job because the boyfriend became progressively more abusive and began to follow her everywhere she went. Only when the stalking escalated did she finally move out of town to find safety.

Causes of Low Self-esteem

Low self-esteem often develops in an environment involving criticism, abuse, or neglect where positive comments are rarely made. The problem usually has its roots in childhood and usually stems from poor parenting.

However, low self-esteem also may result from a perceived failure in a significant area of life or as a result of mistreatment later in life from significant others such as a spouse or boss.

■ High Self-esteem—the Self-assured Person

Scott is a hospital administrator who regularly encourages his staff and his board of directors to give him feedback about how he's doing in his job. Twice every year, he gets the board members and his staff to fill out an attitude survey which lets them describe how they feel about the job environment, about productivity, and about his strengths and weaknesses. Scott easily accepts positive things that are said such as "You have really increased the quality of care for the patient." He's also able to confidently handle negative remarks such as "You let some people perform poorly without taking action." He feels good about himself but is not overly self-critical or vain.

Strengths

The self-assured person is one who scores moderate to high in self-esteem. He genuinely likes himself and has strong self-respect and self-esteem. He is aware of his positive qualities and abilities, yet he can also recognize his faults, inadequacies, and shortcomings. He's free to recognize the need to change, without becoming defensive and denying the need to change. He's able to confidently and comfortably face criticism or rejection from others.

Potential Difficulties

A person who is very high to extremely high on the self-esteem scale can appear to feel good about herself. She tries to feel good about herself by acting superior to others. She may have responded to earlier feelings of inferiority by repressing these feelings and by imagining that she was superior. She may now deny having personal shortcomings and deny the need to improve herself.

Very highly self-assured people are very defensive about their actions. They have difficulty receiving criticism. They are usually unwilling to admit responsibility for a problem related to their actions. Because of their defensiveness, they do not respond well to suggestions that they need to make personal changes. They try to prove they are right even if they are wrong. They may make low status people feel unimportant.

While being very self-assured feels good, it often only covers up feelings of inferiority that really should be addressed. Because excessive self-assurance tends to result in win-lose situations and prevents constructive change, people with this quality should work to change this area of emotional intelligence.

Sean was a legend in his own mind. He had been a moderately successful athlete in his teens and twenties—just good enough to warm the bench on his high school and college teams. His description of his performance, though, made it sound like he was the star player. Now forty years old, he often dressed in sports outfits that made him look like he might still be on the team.

Sean was hard to live with. As a last effort before going to a divorce lawyer, Sean's wife got them into counseling. When Sean was included in the counseling, he was very willing to discuss problems that he thought his wife had. The counselor, by interviewing the whole family, determined that Sean was very critical of his wife and very neglectful. However, during eight weeks of counseling, he never admitted to causing any part of their problems. His wife finally gave up, divorced him, and remarried.

Throughout the counseling, Sean presented himself to the counselor as being a kind and moral person, yet he had often hit his wife and had been convicted at least twice for causing physical fights with other men. He also started a fistfight with his ex-wife's new husband. When the counselor later found out about the fistfights, Sean was not apologetic about failing to provide this information. He said that knowing about the fights was irrelevant since none of them were his fault.

Sean could not work for others. When a boss would give him constructive criticism, he would get very defensive and deny the problems. Sean also had many business failures. He started his own businesses several times, but they never succeeded. He perceived every new business venture as a way of making it big. Every failure was explained away by blaming someone or something else. This kept him from learning from his mistakes.

Causes of High Self-esteem

Moderate to high self-esteem tends to develop in an environment where others demonstrate genuine love and concern for the person. Positive things are said to the person and about the person to others. However, errors, faults, and inadequacies are pointed out in a realistic—yet not harsh—manner.

Very high self-assurance tends to develop in an environment where others were not positive about or were critical of the person, since high estimation of self can be a defense against feeling inferior. These people inwardly like themselves much less than they show the world around them.

More rarely, very high self-assurance results from an environment where the person is told and is treated as if they're better off than others. These "princes" and "princesses" actually believe they are nearly perfect.

■ Identifying Self-esteem

Self-esteem can vary from day to day or year to year. In fact, more people vary in their self-esteem than they do in any other emotional intelligence tendency. Many people feel humble most of the time but can at times also be very self-assured. If you are not careful in your evaluation, you may only find out about how this person is feeling at the time of your meeting with her.

When you simply ask a person to describe herself without further explanation, if she is very humble, you may hear her list few positive characteristics and numerous personal faults. You are also likely to find her exaggerating some of the negative characteristics.

If she is moderate to high in self-esteem, she should have plenty of positive characteristics to share and several negative ones. Positives and negatives with these folks should be realistic and not exaggerated.

If she is very self-assured, she will tend to mention many positive characteristics and very few, if any, negative ones. Positive characteristics may be exaggerated while any negative characteristics will tend to be minimized.

Next, ask her to describe something important that she did very well. Then ask her to describe something important she tried to do but failed at.

If she is very humble, she may be hesitant to tell you about her success and may minimize it. She may seem quite willing to tell you about what she did poorly and may exaggerate how poorly she did.

If she is moderate to high in self-esteem, she should be able to comfortably describe both a success and a failure.

Descriptions of successes and failures should be realistic and not exaggerated.

If she is very self-assured, she will probably have trouble describing the failure and may be boastful about the success. Description of the failure will be minimized, while the success may be exaggerated.

Probably the best way to actually observe signs of self-esteem is to listen to the person talk about herself and her accomplishments as we described above. However, also look at how she treats herself. Self-destructive actions, abuse, or neglect are obviously signs of low self-esteem. Giving oneself privileges and taking care of oneself can be signs of higher self-esteem. You'll hear these people say things that infer, "I'm worth it." Indulging oneself with favors or privileges may be signs of excessive self-esteem. These folks seem to be telling themselves and you, "I deserve the best."

You also may watch to see how the person responds to criticism or rejection. Very humble people tend to be hurt and damaged by criticism and rejection. People who are moderate to high in self-esteem handle criticism or rejection the best. Those who are excessively self-assured tend to respond to criticism or rejection with denial and defensiveness.

Other people, if asked, may be able to tell you about the type of self-esteem indicators above.

■ Solutions to Problems

Self-esteem and Jobs

We have found that low self-esteem, while it is emotionally painful, does not necessarily destroy academic or task-related performance. Many of the best performers have either low or conditional self-esteem.

However, low self-esteem is stressful, limits your happiness, and can put you at risk for developing depression. Therefore, low self-esteem is a problem that should be taken seriously and overcome.

It is generally best to have a moderate to high amount of self-esteem for most circumstances and for most jobs. Excessive self-esteem causes problems with people and prevents emotional improvement.

If a job involves working with people who may be critical or rejecting, a person's degree of self-esteem should be moderate to high. This would apply to sales work, customer service, counseling, teaching, or management positions.

Self-esteem and Relationships

Humble people normally feel more comfortable around and have fewer conflicts with other humble people. They will agree upon modesty and won't offend or intimidate each other by bragging or by vanity. Humble people usually like to be around positive people, who can make them feel better about themselves.

Moderate to high self-assured people are most compatible with others who are similarly self-assured, but they are not incompatible with humble or very self-assured people.

Very self-assured people like to be with other very self-assured people if the other self-assured people include them in their elite group. The elite group also may exclude a group of other people not deemed as important. Very self-assured people can get on each other's nerves if competitiveness for ego superiority is turned toward each other in a battle over who's the best or who is right.

A humble person may initially be attracted to a self-assured person, being captivated or inspired by his or her feelings of importance. The humble person may even feel more important because he is with someone who projects self-importance—especially if the other person is also positive. The very self-assured person may enjoy having a humble companion who makes her feel better off by comparison. A win-lose relationship can develop however, and the humble person may eventually get tired of being the loser.

Over time, the humble person will tend to see the very self-assured person as being too showy and prideful. He may begin to feel inadequate and irritated with very self-assured people who are proud or who look down on others. The very self-assured person may regard the humble person as being too modest. For example, the very self-assured person would tend to want to drive a Mercedes while the humble person may feel more comfortable with a Chevrolet. These conflicts are solvable if any of three things happen:

1) The humble person becomes more self-assured.
2) The very self-assured person becomes more humble.
3) The two people learn to appreciate the value of one being humble and the other self-assured and respect and appreciate one another's unique qualities.

Making the Humble Person Comfortable

To best relate to a humble person, to make him comfortable, and to reduce conflict:

• Provide him with sincere affirmation of his worth and

value, his personal qualities, and his good behaviors—even though he is likely to be slow to accept praise. This praise or affirmation is best done in a low-key, low-profile manner. People with extremely low self-esteem may be very uncomfortable receiving praise.

- Criticism, if any, should be communicated very respectfully and focused only on behavior. A humble person needs freedom from harsh criticism or personal rejection, though he may feel he deserves it. He is more comfortable when there is little need for adjustments of emotional intelligence or when these changes can be made slowly.
- Admit your own shortcomings and faults to him.
- Practice modesty and humility.
- Work to prevent misinterpretation of your actions as rejection or criticism.
- Get others to handle situations that may involve criticism or rejection.
- Place him around other humble people.

Making the Very Self-assured Person Comfortable

To best relate to a very self-assured person to make her comfortable and to reduce conflict:

- Provide her with high status, respect, compliments, approval, prestige, an important position, popularity, public recognition, recognition of position, the opportunity to be seen as a leader, and associations with famous people.
- Give her credit for what she has done well.
- When discussing mistakes, talk only about the actual behavior, the consequences of the behavior, and alternative behaviors. Avoid personal criticism and put-downs.

- Don't expect her to make personal changes or to like criticism of her actions, personal qualities, or accomplishments.
- Don't look down upon her or show disrespect.
- Get others to handle situations that involve low status, criticism, or rejection.

Modifying the Humble Tendency

A friend or counselor could:

1) Listen to his opinion about what he thinks is wrong with him.
2) Restate what the humble person said so he will know the helper understands.
3) Be respectful of his opinion.
4) As much as he is willing, get him to consider the positive side of himself.

Self-help for the Humble Person

Learn to appreciate the value, feelings, and contributions of people with high self-esteem by understanding that people with very high opinions of themselves are usually struggling with the same feelings that you have. Try to be less critical of yourself and recognize the basis for your worth and value. This can be accomplished by taking a personal inventory of valuable qualities and abilities.

- Look for fewer faults and more good about yourself.
- Increase positive self-talk. A helpful sentence to keep in mind is: "What is good or right about me or my behavior?"

- Keep a "self-esteem" log by writing down ten or more positive things about your personal actions or attributes every day.
- Work through past situations that stimulated feelings of inadequacy.
- Improve any present life situation that may be causing a poor self-image. If the humble nature is a reaction to negative environmental circumstances, then improving or correcting these situations can lead to a more positive opinion of self.
- Identify what you don't like about yourself such as your weight or a poor vocabulary, and correct or accomplish things that will make you feel better about yourself.
- Get others to remind you of your value and make realistic compliments (even though you may be somewhat uncomfortable with this). Accept the compliments.
- Confront the need to make a needed personal change. Recognize the value of the change and the problems involved with not changing.

Modifying the Very Self-assured Tendency

A friend or counselor could:

1) Listen to her opinion about what she thinks is good about herself.
2) Restate what she has said so she will know the helper understands.
3) Be respectful of her opinion.
4) As much as she is willing, get her to consider her potential problems, faults, or limitations.

Self-help for the Very Self-assured Person

Learn to appreciate the value of people who are more humble. Very highly self-assured people need to learn the causes of low self-esteem and the value of humility.

People with escesive self-esteem who are compensating for feelings of inferiority with their overt behavior need to recognize the basis for their worth and value. This can be done by taking a personal inventory of valuable qualities and abilities. You also may need to work through past or present situations that make you feel inadequate. Once you have developed a true inner security, you should begin to admit inadequacies and short-comings and start making necessary changes.

Very self-assured people need to identify more of the nega-tive/wrong in their actions and attributes by:

- Asking the question "What is negative or wrong about me or my behavior?"
- Facing and correcting more personal problems.
- Getting others to remind you about problems and faults.
- When confronted with the need to make an important personal change, trying to recognize the value of the change and the problems involved with not changing.
- If the self-assurance is excessive and chronic, then keep a "humble" log. Every day write down ten or more things that you need to improve or do better.

Managing the Humble Person

Emphasize, model, require, and reward positive self-state-ments and facing criticism or rejection. Give rewards for fol-lowing a specific plan for developing his self-esteem.

Consider discipline for lack of positive self-statements, for negative self-statements, or for not working at what he plans to do to improve his self-esteem.

Managing the Very Self-assured Person

Emphasize, model, require, and reward apologies and openness about the need to change. Reward handling criticism or rejection with tact. Also reward showing respect for others, especially those who may be less self-assured.

Get Your Pencil—Checkup Time

To Make This Information Useful to You, You Must Apply It!

1) Write down the type of person you fit best (humble or self-assured).
2) Write down how being this way has helped and any specific problems it has caused.
3) If you have had problems with this area of emotional intelligence, then write down which solutions you will use to improve. Perhaps receive a desired reward for completing steps of your plan and for total completion.
4) Carry out the solutions you choose. Trying to change and repetition will make the action part of your character.

To Improve Relationships or to Help Others

1) Write down the type of person that someone you know fits best.
2) Write down how being this way has helped and any specific problems it has caused.
3) If this person has had problems with this area of emotional intelligence, then write down which solutions you will use to reduce conflict with him or her or to build that person's performance. Perhaps he or she can receive a desired reward for completing steps of the plan and for total completion.
4) If you feel that the person is able and willing to receive this feedback, share your new insight with that person and tell him or her about what you think needs to be done.

Chapter 6

Measuring Commitment to Work

Commitment to work is the tendency to work hard, to get things done, and to take on responsibility. This characteristic of emotional intelligence helps measure how devoted a person is to accomplishing tasks whether on the job or at home.

■ Low Commitment to Work— the Leisurely Person

Lex is a security guard who watches a large office building at night. He's expected to stay in the lobby most of the time, watching the main entrances to the building. Every few hours, he checks the other floors. Much of the time Lex enjoys watching television, looking at a book, or working crossword puzzles. These are all acceptable activities for the job.

Once in a while, a thief tries to break into an office, or an office building tenant is assaulted in the parking lot. Because Lex has at least moderate energy and is also courageous, he rises to the occasion and handles these situations with boldness and determination. After Lex has caught the criminal, turned him over to the police, and completed all the paper-work, he returns to his chair and finishes his book.

Laura is a sixty-five-year-old homemaker. Because she lives with only her husband in a very small home, there is little housework to be done. Laura prepares meals about 50 percent of the time. The rest of the time, she and her husband eat out. Laura spends only a few hours each day working, then concentrates on other interests.

Even though she works very little, Laura is fairly busy and active. She spends her time playing with grandchildren, talking on the phone with friends, playing bridge, and shopping. She and her husband also travel frequently.

Strengths

The leisurely person enjoys taking his or her time at tasks. While other people rush to get to work and may stay late to get everything done, the leisurely person doesn't generally feel pressured or hurried to complete work. Leisurely people value rest and recreation over the accomplishment of tasks. The leisurely person desires an environment that involves:

- Plenty of time for rest or breaks.
- Recreation.
- Time off.
- Fewer hours.
- Lower expectations for quantity of work.

If the leisurely person is middle to high in courage, he may temporarily work very hard to overcome a threatening environmental problem, to beat an opponent, or to accomplish a particularly exciting task. Once the challenge is over, however, he returns to his lower level of productivity.

At first glance, being leisurely may seem similar to being slow-paced, but in fact these two character patterns are very different. A person can have high emotional energy but also have a very low commitment to work. This person would be very active doing things that do not involve productive work or concentrating on tasks.

A person can also have low emotional energy and high commitment to work. This person would stay on task and be very serious about work but would not be able to keep up a fast pace or handle pressure well.

Potential Difficulties

Many leisurely people work only as they must in order to meet their specific needs. They tend to be clock-watchers and look forward to quitting time. If allowed to do so, leisurely people tend to avoid or put off work, work slowly, and get little done within a given period of time. Leisurely people will find ways to take a long time to complete a task—often mixing work with nonproductive activities.

If leisurely people are working as a part of a team, their lower rate of productivity may cause others in the group to have to do work that the leisurely people should have done.

In an environment where hard work or long hours are expected, leisurely people will be dissatisfied with the higher amount of work expected. In this environment, they may get less done than required and take more time than desired to complete tasks. Work not done will typically fall on others.

Leisurely people may disagree with harder working people over the amount of time that should be devoted to work versus play or rest. They may feel that the expectations of harder working people are excessive.

Larry had been retired for several years and was enjoying it. He was finally getting to do just what he wanted to do. He traveled a lot, spent time with friends, and developed an interest in computers. Then he discovered that he had less money saved than he thought he had. He then got a job doing data entry for a computer programming company.

On the job, Larry spent too much time talking to others and interrupting their work. He was always taking time to discuss new computer software that he had bought for entertainment. When he got on the phone, he would stay on far too long. Larry seemed to feel little urgency to get his work completed. He was slow at data entry—not for lack of energy but because he didn't take the work seriously. Many times, others in the office would have to work late to complete some of Larry's work because he had not stayed on task. There were also many occasions when Larry would come in late and would leave early. Larry was just doing his time to get his paycheck. He finally had to be fired.

Causes of Low Commitment to Work

The causes of low work tendencies are very diverse. During critical developmental stages, significant others may not have communicated or modeled the value of working hard. Instead, low work tendencies may have been modeled.

The leisurely person may not have been required to work hard, may not have needed to work hard, or may not have been rewarded for working hard. Or he may not have found work that matched his abilities and interests.

In the past, work may have been used as a punishment or associated with loss, injury, pain, fear, unhappiness, criticism, rejection, suffering, loneliness, or hardship. Low commitment to work can result from poor health or from depression. Depression can have physical/medical causes or may be caused by a negative attitude or harsh circumstances.

■ High Commitment to Work—
the Hardworking Person

Harvey is a neurosurgeon who works in a major metropolitan city. He puts in about fifty to sixty hours a week. Harvey is busy working from the time he arrives in the morning until the time he leaves in the evening. He would really prefer to work about forty-five hours a week but is temporarily working more because of the demands of the group he is in practice with.

Even though he works a lot, Harvey finds time for friends, family, rest, and recreation. When he comes home from work, he plays with his children and talks with his wife. On Saturdays, he plays golf. He exercises moderately throughout the week and gets at least seven hours of sleep each night. At work, he manages to take a couple of breaks during the day despite the fact that people are always waiting to see him.

Strengths
. . . .

Hardworking people spend time productively. They get started on their own and push themselves to finish tasks. Hard workers take on responsibility without others having to prompt them. They work hard, long, and often. They have a strong desire to complete a task or project. Hardworking people get much pleasure from accomplishing tasks—especially those that they personally choose to do. They stay on task and do not waste time. Hard workers are usually trying to accomplish, to achieve, or to produce something. They strongly value work, but if they're balanced, they'll also take time for rest and for fun.

Note that just by knowing that a person is a hard worker, we cannot predict what that person will spend his or her time working on. A neurosurgeon may work tirelessly in surgery but may not take out the trash or cut the grass when he or she gets home. What a person will work on depends upon that person's interests and upon other characteristics of his or her emotional intelligence.

People who score low in desire for change (chapter 8) will like to work on routine tasks such as assembly line work. People who score high in desire for change will not want to do routine work. Instead, they will want to do work that involves variety, new ideas, or new places. Interests partially determine what a person will choose to work on. One person may like to work at landscaping while another person works hard at fixing cars. Still another person may want to work hard at driving a truck.

Potential Difficulties

Extremely hard workers are compulsive about work. They may overload and overstress themselves with tasks. They take little time for rest or for recreation. These people are uncomfortable when they are not being productive.

Even breaks, off-hours, or vacations may be turned into productive pursuits instead of relaxation. Vacations may involve trying to meet a series of deadlines or trying to accomplish as much as possible. Conversations tend to be mostly about work.

Some people can handle excessive hours of work without developing physical problems. However, more often those who work too hard stress their bodies more than is practical, resulting in muscular tension, stomach problems, various sicknesses (due to lower immune responses), or heart failure.

In an environment where little work is expected or allowed, hardworking people will be dissatisfied with the lower amount of work. They may get more done than required and take less time than desired to complete tasks. They may even do tasks that others should do to feel they have accomplished something.

Harold is a missionary. He, along with his wife and two children, has moved to a foreign country to start a church. Harold works seven, twelve-hour days—approximately eighty-four hours a week. During the mornings and afternoons, Harold works a regular eight-hour job to make the money his family needs to live on. Then at night, he works another four hours to build the membership of the church. Saturday and Sunday are totally spent in calling on new church prospects, visiting sick people, fixing the church building, counseling, teaching, preparing his sermon, and preaching.

While this workload would cause many people to develop physical stress-related problems, Harold is able to keep up this pace of work without noticeable symptoms. However, he does look tired and run-down at the end of the day. Harold is happiest when he is working and getting things done. Therefore, the long hours don't seem long to him.

Harold's primary problem is that his wife and children feel totally neglected. Even when the family is together at night, a phone call or a knock at the door can call Harold away from them. He spends no time playing with his children. He feels that he does not have time for play. He also feels that his children should be more serious about work. His children are falling in with a bad crowd in school, are making poorer grades, and are developing a strong bitterness toward their father. They are also developing a negative attitude toward religion. As a result of the lack of attention, Harold's wife has sought out counseling as a last resort before pursuing a divorce.

Causes of High Commitment to Work

During important developmental stages, significant others may have communicated or modeled the value of working hard. The hardworking person may have been required to do excessive work, may have needed to work a lot to meet financial needs, or may have been rewarded for accomplishing tasks. Another contributing factor is that the hardworking person may have found work that exactly matched his or her abilities and interests.

In the past, work may have been associated with reward, gain, profit, comfort, pleasure, happiness, satisfaction, recognition, acceptance, praise, privileges, or friendship.

■ Identifying the Leisurely or Hardworking Person

Ask these people to describe a typical day from the time they get up to the time they go to sleep. Get them to tell you everything they do. Don't tell them what you are looking for. Just keep them talking about what happens and about how they feel.

If they are leisurely, you may find that they:

- Do not look forward to getting to work.
- May be late to work.
- Are slow to get started on tasks.
- Don't give the task their full attention.
- Wander off of the task.
- Do things that are fun when work needs to be done.
- Mix rest or recreation into the accomplishment of a task.
- Have little urgency for getting as much done as they can with their time.
- Don't complete tasks and feel comfortable not completing them.
- Don't mind when things happen that delay the completion of tasks.
- Don't spend many hours actually getting things done.
- Look forward to getting off of work.

If they are hardworking, you may find that they:

- Look forward to getting to work.
- Come to work on time or early.
- Hit the floor running.
- Focus on the task and stay on task even when there are enjoyable distracting options.
- Work when they are supposed to be working and save nonproductive fun for after work hours.
- Strive to get as much done as they can with their time.
- Complete tasks and feel uncomfortable not completing them.

- Dislike it when things happen that delay the completion of tasks.
- Spend many hours actually getting things done.
- May dislike stopping their work for the day.

Next ask them, "If you won $10 million, what would you do?" Let them explain in detail. Listen to see if they would still work. How much or how often? Hard workers would work, even if they didn't need the money.

After getting them to express themselves in such an open-ended manner, you can then ask more specific questions. Be careful. These questions are much more obvious than the open-ended ones, and some people will be able to tell what you are looking for. Some more specific questions could be: What time does your office open? What time do you typically arrive at work? When was the last time you were late? Why did you come in late? Why do you come in on time?

When you arrive at work, how long is it before you are getting something important done? What are you doing when you are not starting your tasks? How do you feel about what you are doing? How do you feel about getting started to work?

When you start a task, do you typically stay at it until it is done, or do you stop and start? Do you find yourself starting a task and then wandering off to do other things that are more enjoyable?

How do you feel when you have not gotten much done with your time? If you are expected to have a task finished by a certain time, do you usually get it done on time? How do you feel when you don't get your task done on time?

Think about when you were working on a task that was significant to the work you do. How did you feel when someone delayed you? How many hours of work do you do each day? Out of all the hours you are at work, how many hours do you spend actually accomplishing your work?

How do you feel about going to work? Would you rather not go? How do you feel about leaving work for the day? Would you rather stay? When you are off the clock, do you find yourself thinking about how to accomplish things at work?

■ Solutions to Problems

Leisurely and Hard Workers on the Job

It is generally best to have a moderate to high amount of commitment to work for most circumstances and for most jobs. Leisurely people, just as they are, can fit well into some relaxed job environments such as night watchmen, nursing home aids, or lifeguards. In some of these relaxed jobs, a very hardworking individual would be less qualified because of that person's frustration with the periodic lack of activity.

Hardworking people are a better fit for most job settings and most interpersonal relationships. An organization full of hardworking people is usually highly productive. Our whole country benefits by the efforts of hard workers in every type of service from political, military, and religious workers to entertainers, medical, or sanitation workers.

Extremely hard workers probably do more than their fair share. In most cases, they work harder than is really necessary, often at the expense of their health and of important relationships.

Commitment to Work and Relationships

Leisurely people normally feel more comfortable around and have fewer conflicts with other leisurely people. Leisurely people tend to agree on how many hours should be worked and how much time for rest or recreation there should be. Hardworking people also tend to agree with each other about how much time should be spent working versus playing.

A leisurely person may be attracted to a hardworking person out of respect for how much he or she gets done. A hardworking person also may enjoy the leisurely person if he or she is also fun-loving and helps her or him to have fun. However, there is a tendency over time for leisurely and hardworking people to develop conflicts.

Leisurely people tend to dislike the overemphasis they believe hardworking people have about getting things done. They may not like the pressure that hardworking people put on them to accomplish. Leisurely people will also want to rest or play more than the hardworking person is willing to do.

Hardworking people may be displeased with the lack of accomplishment of those who score low on the commitment to work scale and tend to feel that this low work level is immature. If the hardworking person already has enough to do, he or she may be displeased with having to do some of the leisurely person's tasks.

If the hard worker works outside of the home, those at home may dislike the amount of time he or she spends away from the family. This is particularly true if the jobholder is an extremely hard worker. This family conflict also tends to be worsened if those at home are not hardworking or if they are emotionally dependent.

These conflicts are solvable if any of three things happen:

1) The leisurely person can become more hardworking.

2) The hardworking person can become more leisurely.

3) The two people can learn to appreciate the value of one being leisurely and the other hard working. They can also respect and appreciate one another's unique qualities.

Making the Leisurely Person Comfortable

To best relate to leisurely people, to make them comfortable and to reduce conflict:

- Provide plenty of time for rest and recreation.
- Allow time off.
- Schedule fewer hours.
- Let them work for shorter periods, alternating with periods for rest or fun.
- Lower expectations of quantity.
- Let them mix work with doing things they enjoy.
- Choose work for them that's in line with their abilities, interests, and emotional intelligence.

While the following suggestions will make leisurely people feel comfortable, they are not normally advisable in a work setting. Let them:

- Come in late to work.
- Get started when they want to.
- Do things that are fun when work needs to be done.
- Leave tasks unfinished.

- Get off of work early.
- Take plenty of time off.
- Let others handle situations where working long hours is important.
- Put them around other leisurely people.

Making the Hardworking Person Comfortable

To best relate to hardworking people, to make them comfortable, and to reduce conflict, give them:
- A fast work pace.
- Low to moderate time for rest and recreation.
- Moderate to long hours.
- Low to moderate time off.
- High expectations of quantity.
- Appreciation for their time spent working and for what was accomplished.
- Hardworking coworkers.

Modifying the Leisurely Tendency

A friend or counselor could:
1) Listen to their opinion about what they think is wrong with hard work.
2) Restate what leisurely people say so they will know the helper understands.
3) Be respectful of their opinion.
4) As much as they are willing, get them to consider the value of hard work.

Self-help for the Leisurely Person

- Learn to appreciate the value, feelings, and contributions of people with high commitment to work.
- Rest/recreate less.
- Try to stay on task.
- Work harder, faster, longer, or more often.
- Commit yourself to do things that need to be done. Follow through.
- Value work more.
- Set life goals and see how the work is needed to get there.
- If you are tired, have your health and fitness evaluated by a physician and, if indicated, follow directions for the proper diet, exercise, and medicine.
- If the low work tendency is a result of depression, and if the depression is not physically based, then the development of a positive attitude or correcting adverse life situations will help.
- Keep a "work attitude" log. Each day before work, spend at least ten minutes considering what you will be doing and write down what is good about completing each task. Write down how it will benefit you and how it will help you to reach your career goals or other major goals.

Modifying the Hardworking Tendency

A friend or counselor could:

1) Listen to their opinion about what they think is good or necessary about working a lot.

2) Restate what they have said so they will know the helper understands.

3) Be respectful of their opinion.

4) As much as they are willing, get them to consider potential problems with working too much. Also get them to consider the value of rest and recreation.

Self-help for the Hardworking Person

- Learn to appreciate the value of people who are leisurely and the causes of being leisurely.

- Constructively deal with compulsive ideas such as "I will only be safe/secure if I work excessively," "I am only good when I do something productive," and "I must work extremely hard to provide what I need to be happy and fulfilled."

- Examine the basis for the compulsion to accomplish.

- If you are working excessively to meet real needs (e.g., financial) find a way to meet these needs with less work.

- Learn to accept rest and play.

- Rest and play more.

- Develop nonwork activities that are rewarding and which compete with the excessive desire to work.

- Budget more time for family and friends.

- Get capable people to do more of the work.

- Work less hard, fast, long, and often.

- Take breaks during the day, week, month, and year and don't turn them into productive achievements.

- Be sure to take care of your health through appropriate rest, diet, and exercise.

- Keep a "rest and play" attitude log. Each day before work, spend at least ten minutes considering what you will do for rest or for fun that day. Write down what is good about each restful or fun activity. Write down how it will benefit you. Write down how it is reasonable and right to pursue rest or fun.

Managing the Leisurely Person

Get others to remind the person to begin, continue, and finish work. Emphasize, model, require, and reward working more. Reward for self-starting, staying on task, and completing work, according to the degree of accomplishment. Let that person experience the natural consequences of his or her lack of work. Consider discipline for lack of productivity or for nonworking behavior.

Managing the Hardworking Person

Get others to remind the person to take breaks, slow down, and take time off when appropriate. Emphasize, model, require, and reward resting or playing more. Consider discipline for excessive work or for lack of rest or play.

■ Get Your Pencil—Checkup Time

To Make This Information Useful to You, You Must Apply It!

1) Write down the type of person you fit best (leisurely or hardworking).
2) Write down how being this way has helped and any specific problems it has caused.
3) If you have had problems with this area of emotional intelligence, then write down which solutions you will use to improve. Perhaps receive a desired reward for completing steps of your plan and for total completion.
4) Carry out the solutions you choose. Trying to change and repetition will make the action part of your character.

To Improve Relationships or to Help Others

1) Write down the type of person that someone you know fits best.
2) Write down how being this way has helped and any specific problems it has caused.
3) If that person has had problems with this area of emotional intelligence, then write down which solutions you will use to reduce conflict with him or her or to build that person's performance. Perhaps he or she can receive a desired reward for completing steps of the plan and for total completion.
4) If you feel that the person is able and willing to receive this feedback, share your new insight with that person and tell him or her about what you think needs to be done.

Chapter 7

Measuring Attention to Detail

Attention to detail measures to what degree a person pays careful attention to what he or she is doing. This measurement of emotional intelligence also indicates to what degree a person strives for precision in tasks. High attention to detail is a very important personal characteristic. Along with commitment to work, it makes up what is known as the work ethic.

■ Low Attention to Detail— the Spontaneous Person

Scott is a very successful manufacturer's sales representative, selling cleaning chemicals to laundries. His product line is brief and uncomplicated, and he has been well trained on the products and how to best present them. When selling, Scott has to do a lot of quick thinking on his feet. If one method of selling doesn't seem to be working with a given client, he must quickly change his tactics. Every day, Scott has to be at a variety of customer locations and meet many different people. He's with each customer for just a few minutes and then is off to visit another one. The home office provides him with assistance and price quotes and follows up to see that orders reach clients on time. Even though Scott has low attention to detail, it does not cause him significant difficulty in this nontechnical sales job.

Strengths

Because they don't get bogged down with excessive detail, spontaneous people reach conclusions and take action quickly. This style can be advantageous, especially if a person has had previous experience with the task. Spontaneous people are intuitive. They are guided by and act on their feelings or hunches. As generalists, spontaneous people see the big picture and prefer to operate based upon a general or basic understanding. They do best with uncomplicated, nondetailed, short-term tasks. Bottom-line oriented, they prefer summaries to complex material. They are broadly focused, typically liking a variety of tasks and activities. They have the ability to do a job or task, feel that it was done well enough, and move on to the next task.

Potential Difficulties

Spontaneous people are short on concentration and attention span. They don't like to focus their attention on a single task for long periods of time. They're easily distracted by other stimuli such as noise or conversation.

They may be imprecise. To them, physical movement that is close, is close enough. For example, a spontaneous person who works on cars probably would not use a torque wrench to make sure that the bolts are tightened perfectly. A spontaneous person would normally not make a good watch repairman or diamond cutter because of the need for physical precision in those jobs.

Spontaneous people tend to learn only the basics of a subject or task. They don't normally try to learn all aspects of complex subjects or tasks. They usually don't study or research a subject in depth. In school, spontaneous people would be the ones in line to buy the Cliff Notes so they could skip reading the entire text of a book.

Spontaneous people are not thorough and may not complete all the parts of a detailed task. A spontaneous person who waxes a car misses spots. A spontaneous taxpayer may not itemize deductions even though it could save a lot of money. Watch out for spontaneous medical doctors who don't study your problems well enough to arrive at an accurate diagnosis. If they work with complex data, spontaneous people may tend to be inaccurate, not because they cannot calculate correctly, but because of careless errors.

Spontaneous people tend to be error-prone and accident-prone. A spontaneous driver may pull out into the path of another car because he or she wasn't concentrating. Spontaneous people would be prone to leaving an iron on at home, knocking a glass off of a table, putting a foot under a lawn mower, overmedicating a patient, and dragging an electrical cord into a water puddle. You wouldn't want a spontaneous person working around a table saw.

Spontaneous people are often disorganized. Unless they have assistance, their living or work area will tend to be messy.

They may have trouble finding things. They'll also forget things like appointments and deadlines.

They tend to act before they think through what they are going to do. Their decisions can be impulsive and hasty. They may say or do things quickly based on a feeling before evaluating the consequences. While spontaneous people are intuitive, they often may not know the logical basis for their conclusions. This can cause them to make poor decisions if they have not had much training in an area. Spontaneous people tend to skip from one activity to another without completing them. In conversation, they'll go off on tangents and change subjects rather frequently.

Don't assume that every spontaneous person will have trouble in school or understanding complex subjects. Some spontaneous people can have very high intelligence and can perform better than you might predict. These are the people who seldom study but make great (not necessarily perfect) grades. Because of their unusually high intelligence, these people can learn from a minimum of study or instruction.

It's possible that a person who often *behaves* spontaneously may actually be trying very hard to be careful. For example, a person with Attention Deficit Disorder (ADD) may actually value doing things well and try hard to concentrate on what he or she is doing. However, the ADD brain dysfunction will cause the person to lose focus and to become distracted, making him or her look like a truly spontaneous person when in fact that isn't true. Without treatment, this person will suffer greatly because of not being able to do what he or she really values doing.

One spontaneous act that I will never forget occurred at the hospital when my third son was born. After delivery in the operating room, the baby was brought into the recovery room where my wife and many family members were waiting. The nurse brought in the baby, put it into my wife's arms, and left the room. Everyone in the room oohed and aahed over the baby. My wife was so pleased to hold it. It was a joyous occasion, except for one thing.

I didn't recognize the baby. It didn't look like the one I had held in the operating room. When I looked at the identification bracelet, I was shocked to find another family's name there. The bracelet was also pink because this baby was a girl. However, my wife had delivered a boy. The nurse brought us the wrong baby and had taken our baby to other parents!

The television sitcom *Home Improvement* gives many exaggerated but colorful examples of extremely spontaneous behavior. On each episode, Tim Taylor, the host of a show about tools and a very spontaneous person, makes hilarious blunders such as accidentally breaking pipes by knocking a hole in a wall, getting his shirt ripped off because it was too close to a table saw, and blowing up a house by not being careful with a gas stove.

When Tim walks down the stairs that lead to his basement, he always hits his head on the same particular pipe. He has so many accidents that the doctors and nurses in the emergency room all know him on a first-name basis.

Tim's accidents actually involve the operation of several character traits besides low attention to detail. Tim has a very high amount of courage (chapter 9) and is, therefore, not afraid to take risks. He tries to do things that are very challenging. He is driven by his needs for self-esteem (chapter 5) to do things that will get attention from others. He probably also has an excessive desire for change (chapter 8) and is very comfortable making decisions (chapter 10).

Causes of Low Attention to Detail

Children are born spontaneous and have to become influenced by their environment to become more detailed. You could say that being spontaneous is the natural way to be. When a person has very low attention to detail, he or she probably grew up in an environment where there was little emphasis on doing things carefully. Thoroughness and accuracy may not have been modeled, required, or rewarded.

Low attention to detail also may have developed in an environment where no performance was ever good enough to succeed or to please those in control. Thus, the person may have just given up on trying to do things well.

The spontaneous person may never have found tasks that fit his or her abilities, interests, or emotional intelligence. Attention to detail will usually decrease if a person is depressed. Some people are spontaneous due to having Attention Deficit Disorder (ADD), which involves a specific brain dysfunction and is often directly inherited from one or both parents.

■ High Attention to Detail—the Careful Person

Ralph is a pharmacist. Ralph reads the doctor's prescription and provides the patient with the correct medication in the correct strength and in the correct amount. An error could be fatal to the patient, so Ralph must be extremely accurate and precise, following only approved pharmaceutical methods. Ralph fills one prescription at a time and generally serves one person at a time. Ralph keeps all medications, tools, reference materials, etc., in their place. He also runs the cash register and must be accurate in charging and in collecting money.

Strengths

Careful people strive to do quality work and try to be accurate, careful, precise, neat, and thorough. They enjoy doing precision work. They tend to be on time and want to work in an environment where there is an emphasis on and recognition of quality work.

Careful people want to have the time and resources necessary to do things right. They like to know what is expected of them so they can be sure to do the correct thing. They want to use methods that are proven to be effective and then check the accuracy of their work before depending upon it.

Careful people are also usually studious and are willing to try to learn complex material. They will prepare thoroughly to avoid failing and ideally want to have the time to learn something before doing it.

Careful people like to steadily build their skills over a long period of time and tend to develop specialized skills and knowledge. Experts will typically be careful people. Careful people have usually learned the value of structuring their thoughts, tasks, and environments so that they can perform as well as possible. Thus, they tend to be methodical, systematic, logical, and organized.

The work area of a careful person is easy to spot. It's organized so that everything needed can be easily found and used. Work and living areas will normally be neat and clean.

Careful people usually make decisions step by step. They tend to think through their decisions and want plenty of time to decide or to plan. Careful people concentrate well and focus their attention. They prefer to complete one task before going to the next one. They want to finish what is started. Their conversations tend to stay on the same subject until it's fully discussed.

Careful people may not do as many routine or boring details if they also have a high to very high desire for change (chapter 8). The careful person who is also change-oriented may put off doing boring details and yet concentrate on doing new tasks very well.

Potential Difficulties

Very careful people have trouble delegating responsibility because they tend to be doers not delegators. They're more comfortable doing a task themselves so that it can be done right. If they do delegate, they may later try to do the task themselves, if they feel it's not being done as well as they would do it.

Very careful people tend to strongly dislike being interrupted when they are working. They can become engrossed with the finite details of a task and forget the big picture. They are like a person who stands so close to a wall that they can only see what is in front of their nose. An extremely careful person may continue to polish the brass while the boat sinks.

They may try to do some tasks better than is practical, while other important priorities receive too little attention. They tend to develop a narrow scope of tasks or activities. Like most people, very careful people have hunches or feelings, but they don't act on them unless there is factual data to rely upon. They may be overly deliberate when making decisions.

Carla was a mother of four children who still managed to keep an immaculate house. Everything was in its place, clean and dust-free. She never let her children help with the housework, which she regarded as being her job. She also believed that she could do any of the household chores better than anyone else and that the children would only make mistakes.

When her children would try to make up a bed, she would act very displeased, pull the covers off, and do it the way she liked it to be done. Her children were not allowed to do any work in the kitchen—this was Carla's most important place to work. If they wanted something to eat, Carla made it for them. Then Carla cleaned the table, washed the dishes, and put them away. Carla seemed irritable when others would leave something out of place but would always be the one to put it back in place.

Carla had what I would call a "perfect room." This was a sitting room, where all of her most perfect furniture was placed. It was like a display window at a department store—only on rare occasions could anyone go into this room.

As you might imagine, none of Carla's children learned to pick up after themselves or to cook. The girls did begin to cook after they got married, although they had trouble believing they could do it well enough. The daughter who made the most money tended to eat out a lot and found a husband who liked to cook, while the daughter who made less money tried to cook simple things she felt would not fail. Carla's boys simply married women whom they expected to be like their mother. The wives, however, were not just like Carla, which caused a good bit of fighting.

Chuck is a general practitioner physician in private practice. He's the type of doctor who will take time to listen to all of his patients' complaints. He carefully gathers all available information before making a diagnosis. Instead of guessing about causes of disorders, he'll run extensive tests. His patients feel that he cares about them and that he understands their problems.

However, because he is excessively careful, Chuck takes a very long time to make a diagnosis. Some patients are annoyed because they feel that he runs tests that are not necessary. When he decides on a course of action, he rethinks it several times. His perfectionism makes decisions very stressful for him.

Patients also complain that they have to wait too long before they see the doctor. On a typical day, a person with an appointment at 1 P.M. may not get to see Chuck until 2 or even 3 P.M. because he spends so much time with patients. He is only able to treat about half as many patients as most doctors do because of his slow, extremely cautious behavior.

In his office, Chuck has stacks of paperwork that are not complete because he feels he needs to be the one to do the work even though in most practices a nurse or office worker fills out these forms.

Causes of High Attention to Detail

During formative years, careful people typically were exposed to a high emphasis on doing things well. Thoroughness and accuracy were modeled, required, or rewarded. Perfectionism also may develop in an environment where accuracy and thoroughness were the only ways to meet basic needs for health, approval, and happiness. For example, a person may develop perfectionism on a job where perfection is demanded and the person cannot afford to lose the job.

When children are only given respect if they are highly accomplished, perfectionism often develops. This conditional respect can also have the opposite effect, leading some children to give up and not try to achieve at all.

■ Identifying Attention to Detail

Ask a person to describe how he or she accomplished a complex task. If you're interviewing the person for a job, the task should be one that is relevant to the job. As always, don't let the person know what you are looking for and keep her talking.

If she is spontaneous, the actual verbal description of the task may be lacking in detail. She may wander off the subject during the conversation. There may be evidence of not preparing well or studying before attempting the task. You may be able to tell that she was not careful, rushed the completion of the task, did not make use of the right tools, left out steps, or did not do the whole task.

If she is careful, the verbal description of the task will tend to be detailed. People like this tend to stay on the subject of the conversation without wandering off on tangents. There may be evidence of preparing well or studying before attempting the task. You'll probably be able to tell that she was careful, took her time, made sure she had the right tools, took careful steps, and completed the whole task.

If she is excessively careful, her description will be very detailed. Her preparation and behavior will seem exaggerated. You may be able to tell that she took too much time to do the job or did the task much better than was practical, such as painting a house so carefully that no mistakes would be visible even with a magnifying glass.

Next, ask if she did the task well? If she did or didn't do it well, how did she feel about it?

Spontaneous people often don't feel bad about doing a task poorly. They also may not feel a great deal of satisfaction from doing it well. Careful people, however, feel a sense of accomplishment when they do something well and dislike not doing well. Extremely careful people feel very bad about doing a task poorly and may even be angry with themselves.

■ Solutions to Problems

Attention to Detail and Jobs
· ·

Being spontaneous is great for a variety of nondetailed careers including abstract art, nontechnical sales, many professional sports, and nondetailed production work or service.

Due to the possibility of increased error, it's generally recommended that spontaneous people do not pursue careers in high-detail areas such as surgery, watch repair, computer programming, or accounting.

As the world has become more complex, attention to detail has become a basic necessity for survival or success. Jobs have generally become more complicated and technical. Being a salesperson used to be fairly simple. Now most salespeople must have plenty of technical knowledge about their products.

Attention to detail can determine the popularity or usefulness of most products or services. Examples are banking, food preparation, and clothing or furniture making. Attention to detail has made Asian companies number one in electronics sales. It's only through increasing attention to detail that American automobile manufacturers have been able to continue to compete with the Japanese and European manufacturers.

Some personal tasks, such as balancing a checkbook or figuring taxes, have always required some attention to detail. Now, however, you must possess attention to detail to program your VCR or to work on your computer-controlled automobile.

Because of our increasingly technical environment, most people now need to have at least moderate attention to detail to successfully cope with both job and personal demands.

Attention to Detail and Relationships

Spontaneous people normally feel more comfortable around and have fewer conflicts with other spontaneous people. They tend to agree on minimal preparation before doing a task, taking as little time as possible to do it, not needing the best tools, and on doing a task only as well as it has to be done. Since spontaneous people like to change subjects frequently in conversation, they'll prefer to talk with other spontaneous people.

While everyone in a work group may be more comfortable with each other if they are all spontaneous, they may eventually find that they need a careful person to handle details. A spontaneous business entrepreneur may need a careful administrative assistant and a careful vice president of finance. An outside salesperson who is spontaneous may appreciate having assistance with details from the home office.

Similarly, careful people normally feel more comfortable around and have fewer conflicts with other careful people. They tend to agree on preparing before doing a task, taking the time to do something right, having the tools that will improve the outcome of tasks, and on doing a task well or very well. Careful people will want to stay on the same subject longer in conversation and may prefer to talk with other careful people.

A spontaneous person may be very attracted to a careful person because the careful person is so neat, organized, and productive. A careful person may be attracted to a spontaneous person's spontaneity and quickness in decision making. However, over time, spontaneous and careful people tend to develop conflicts.

Spontaneous people are uncomfortable with those who maintain a higher concern for detail. They may feel the expectations of the high-detail person are excessive and unreasonable. Conflicts will inevitably arise over how well a task should be done to be considered finished.

Careful people will also have conflicts with spontaneous people. The careful person tends to view the spontaneous person as too careless, while the spontaneous person tends to view the careful person as too compulsive or picky.

These conflicts are solvable if any of three things happen:

1) The spontaneous person can become more careful.

2) The careful person can become less detail-oriented.

3) The two people can learn to appreciate the value of one being spontaneous and the other being careful. They can learn to respect and appreciate one another's unique qualities.

Making the Spontaneous Person Comfortable

To best relate to spontaneous people, to make them comfortable, and to reduce conflict, let them:

- Act on their feelings and impulses.
- Do tasks that are simple, short-term, and not complex.
- Have a variety of things to do.
- Change the subject in conversations.
- Start on another task when they have exhausted their concentration on a task.
- Learn the basics and then do them.
- Learn by doing.
- Have protection from distractions.
- Have protection from accidents.
- Do tasks that require lower precision.
- Be with other spontaneous people.
- Get others to research, study, provide summaries, organize, and handle situations where being detailed is important.

Making the Careful Person Comfortable

To best relate to careful people, to make them comfortable, and to reduce conflict, let them:

- Make decisions based upon facts and less upon feelings or guesses.
- Do tasks that are detailed, long-term, or complex.
- Stay on the subject in conversations without jumping around.
- Focus their concentration on completing their task.
- Prepare well and study before attempting a new task.
- Build their skills over time.
- Take the time needed to do the job right.
- Get recognition for their good work.
- Know what is expected of them.
- Have the tools or resources that help them to do well.
- Work in an organized setting.
- Complete the task and do it well.
- Check their own work.
- Be around other careful people.

With extremely careful people, follow the suggestions for the careful person and also let them:

- Be a doer not a delegator.
- Be a do-it-yourselfer.
- Focus only on one task at a time.
- Have protection from interruptions.
- Get others to handle situations that involve fast decision making, delegating responsibility, or handling a variety of tasks.

- Others could remind the extremely careful person of priorities, expectations, and deadlines.

Modifying the Spontaneous Tendency

A friend or counselor could:
1) Listen to their opinion about what they think is wrong with precision or detail in their work.
2) Restate what they have said so they will know the helper understands.
3) Be respectful of their opinion.
4) As much as they are willing, get them to consider what is good about practicing precision or detail.

Self-help for the Spontaneous Person

- Appreciate the value, feelings, and contributions of people with high attention to detail.
- Concentrate and pay more attention to detail.
- Focus on the task, pushing out other thoughts.
- Be more precise, reflective, thorough, methodical, systematic, logical, accurate, careful, safety-minded, organized, neat, and punctual.
- Value, learn, and do details.
- Develop and continually follow a practical system for the placement of things, for scheduling time, and for methods for the accomplishment of tasks.
- Be more studious, emphasizing the importance of the information.
- Learn complex material.
- Think through decisions and plan steps before acting.

- Stay on the task until it is complete.
- Talk to yourself about what you need to do as you complete each step of the task.
- Maintain more focus in conversations.
- Calculate risk, difficulty, or danger to prevent loss, injury, or hardship.
- Find tasks that are interesting enough to motivate you to concentrate.
- Use massed or repetitive practice to improve the performance of specific tasks.
- Keep a "detail" log and every day consider several things that need to be done well, then write down what is good or positive about doing them well and consider the benefits.
- If you are depressed, seek treatment for depression.
- If the depression is a reaction to a loss or lack of reward, do what can be done to change the circumstance.

Modifying the Extremely Careful Tendency

This section is designed to help people who are either extremely careful or who are simply too careful for their particular job.

A friend or counselor could:

1) Listen to their opinion about what they think is good about being very careful in their work.
2) Restate what they have said so they will know the helper understands.
3) Be respectful of their opinion.
4) As much as they are willing, get them to consider potential problems involved in being too careful (e.g., taking too much time).

Self-help for the Extremely Careful Person

- Appreciate the value of people who have less attention to detail.
- Stay aware of priorities.
- Leave well-enough alone.
- Share or delegate tasks more.
- Stop taking tasks back.
- Find people who do things well enough to trust them.
- Make decisions faster.
- Act faster by deliberating less.
- Act on hunches when necessary or when no objective data can be found.
- Keep up with a wider scope of activity.
- Work on more than one thing at a time.
- Be less focused in conversations.
- Have more patience with people who don't do things the "right" way.
- See the good that has been done and communicate it.
- Let others learn by trial and error.
- Set realistic expectations for tasks, people, things, and situations.
- Quit spending excessive time preparing for a task.
- Prepare normally for tasks, complete them, and give yourself credit for what was done well.
- Value yourself and your work even when it isn't perfect.
- Recognize that mistakes or limitations are normal and are to be expected.
- Recognize that mistakes are a necessary part of learning, and a person who is not making mistakes is a person who is not growing or developing.

Managing the Spontaneous Person

Check the spontaneous person's plans or work for correctness. Emphasize, model, require, and reward attention to detail. Consider discipline for lack of effort, accuracy, or completion.

Managing the Extremely Careful Person

Emphasize, model, require, and reward faster decisions and action. Consider discipline for too much time spent trying to do a task better than it needs to be done or for not meeting deadlines.

■ Get Your Pencil—Checkup Time

To Make This Information Useful to You, You Must Apply It!

1) Write down the type of person you fit best (spontaneous or careful).

2) Write down how being this way has helped and any specific problems it has caused.

3) If you have had problems with this area of emotional intelligence, then write down which solutions you will use to improve. Perhaps receive a desired reward for completing steps of your plan and for total completion.

4) Carry out the solutions you choose. Trying to change and repetition will make the action part of your character.

To Improve Relationships or to Help Others

1) Write down the type of person that someone you know fits best.

2) Write down how being this way has helped and any specific problems it has caused.

3) If that person has had problems with this area of emotional intelligence, then write down which solutions you will use to reduce conflict with him or her or to build that person's performance. Perhaps he or she can receive a desired reward for completing steps of the plan and for total completion.

4) If you feel that the person is able and willing to receive this feedback, share your new insight with that person and tell him or her about what you think needs to be done.

Chapter 8

Measuring Desire for Change

Desire for change measures to what degree people like change in their environment, in what they believe, or in their behavior.

■ Low Desire for Change—the Routine Person

Ruth is an elementary school teacher. She gets up at 6:30 every morning and dresses in the same style of clothes she has worn for twenty years. She usually has a bowl of Raisin Bran with a glass of orange juice for breakfast. She drives to work in a car she's had for many years, using a familiar route. Ruth is an excellent first-grade teacher. She teaches basic skills to children the same way she has since she got out of school herself. After all, two plus two always equals four. A is always followed by B and C.

Strengths

Routine people desire little change in themselves and in the environment around them. In general, they want to keep things the same.

They have the ability to appreciate the way things are and tend not to make impractical changes. They like following set routines and are well suited for jobs that involve following patterns. They tend to be traditional—wanting to stick with standards that have become well known to them. They also enjoy doing things according to schedules. They want standard operating methods and procedures and enjoy repetition. They enjoy using skills and knowledge already learned more than learning something new.

A consistent and predictable environment is best for routine people. They want to go to the same restaurants, grocery stores, or offices day after day. In their home or office, they like for everything to be in its place. They'll typically wear the same types of clothes, read the same types of books, and drive the same types of cars.

Job security is very important to routine people. If possible, they like to keep the same job with the same company, usually in the same geographical location for many years. This serves to make them more of a long-term employee, which can contribute to their company having lower turnover costs.

Routine people strongly want sameness in the people they are around. They want others to look and behave the way they always have.

Potential Difficulties

Very routine people experience anxiety and sometimes even disorientation when they have to make significant changes. They are comfortable in a rut and will try to keep things the same even when a change would be better. They may try to hold on to things that have outlived their practical usefulness.

Very routine people may try to perform in familiar but less effective ways that have already been improved upon. In trying to maintain security, they tend to hold on to tasks that they have frequently performed even if they are tasks that belonged to their previous job position. They'll turn down promotions or transfers, even if the new position offers better pay and benefits.

Predictably, routine people don't want to determine changes to be made or to institute changes. Their routine character trait tends to stifle creativity. Very routine people need time for preparation to make any significant change.

Rusty was an industrial mechanic who worked for a large laundry service. His job involved installing and maintaining industrial-sized washers and dryers and moving clothes racks. Every day for forty years, he got up at exactly 6 A.M. and did a routine of exercises that he learned when he was in the army. After eating a piece of toast, he drove to work the way he always did and parked in the same spot. At work, he continued on a regular maintenance schedule. Each machine was due for inspection and adjustment after a certain number of days in service.

For decades, Rusty ate a ham sandwich for lunch every day. He also wore the same type of clothes. He would wear the same pair of shoes until they had holes in the bottom. When his wife would finally convince him to get a new pair, he'd buy the same style.

Rusty also drove old cars, not because he couldn't afford a new one but because he liked what he knew. He kept his old car even though the newer cars got better gas mileage, went farther between tune-ups, were more comfortable, and were safer.

Eventually, Rusty was offered the job of maintenance supervisor, with a significant increase in pay. However, he turned down the promotion because the duties were different, and that made him feel uncomfortable.

Rusty continued to do a very good job as a mechanic except for dealing with the new technology. He was very reluctant to begin to use new electronic instruments to determine problems with the newer machines. He felt that the old machines were better than what he called the "newfangled contraptions."

Rusty was falling behind the times. During the last part of his career, his boss allowed him to focus his work on the many older machines that were still in service. As soon as he could, he retired, even though mentally and physically he still had many years of work left in him.

Causes of Low Desire for Change

Routine character develops in a very structured environment where routine was emphasized, modeled, required, and rewarded. Creativity or change may have been discouraged or at least not encouraged.

Sometimes a low desire for change develops when there was too much change in someone's life or when someone was hurt by change. These people seek security by keeping things the same. Very low change can be a method of developing feelings of predictability, security, and safety in a very threatening environment.

■ High Desire for Change— the Change-oriented Person

Charley is a gourmet chef. He loves to make different foods in different ways and regards his dishes as creations. When he is developing a new recipe, he works tirelessly until the dish is a success. He gets bored with simply producing a standard meal that has been prepared many times before. Sometimes his creations are a little too creative and don't work—such as the time he tried a new way to make flaming ice cream and it turned into scorched milk.

Mark is a computer programmer. A client tells Mark what he needs the computer to do for him, and Mark makes it happen. At any one time, Mark has at least ten different clients whom he is doing work for. He must travel to each client site to load his programs into the computers. While there is plenty of development and creativity involved in programming, Mark must also do routine work like typing in standard commands. He must also keep records so that he knows where he is with each of his projects.

Strengths
....

Change-oriented people thrive upon variety in their environment. They want new and improved activities and like to travel, seeking a change of settings. They also want much change in tasks, methods, procedures, times for activities, and in the people they are around. Because they like change and are conditioned to it, they adjust easily to changing situations.

Change-oriented people become excited by new tasks and increase their motivation while the task is new and interesting.

Change-oriented people have creative ideas. Because they like to improve things, change-oriented people want to be in jobs where they have the opportunity to be imaginative or creative. They seek visual or intellectual stimulation from their environment, are curious, and open to new ideas.

Making progress in their career is very important to change-oriented people. They like to move up and out. They also like to acquire money and new possessions.

Potential Difficulties

Very change-oriented people dislike routine or mundane tasks and repetition. Because they find it difficult to do the same task over and over again, they are not well suited for jobs that involve following set patterns.

They may seek to change things that don't need improvement or may change things instead of doing less interesting work. They may get bored with routine, neglect routine tasks, and do new, impractical things.

Change-oriented people dislike environments that are too consistent and predictable. Standard operating methods and procedures are not for them. They don't like to go to the same places or locations, and they dislike things always being in the same places. If high-change people can't satisfy their need for change in a given environment, they'll want to find another environment to meet their needs.

Change-oriented people strongly dislike sameness in the people they are around. They dislike being around the same people and want them to look and to behave differently than they have in the past.

Even if keeping things the same would be better, these people will want to change it. They may try to get new things when current things would be better or more practical. They avoid performing in familiar, effective ways and try new things that are not yet proven. They may begin to do tasks that are beyond their job description.

The behavior of change-oriented people is often balanced or controlled by circumstances or by other character traits within the person. For example, a change-oriented person with little money may not keep buying new things, even though he or she may want to do so. A change-oriented surgeon, who is also responsible, may not try a new surgical technique until some proof of its effectiveness has been demonstrated.

Calvin was the president of a huge manufacturing company. He had successfully run the company for ten years when his son had a fatal accident. Calvin's wife was crushed by the loss of her son and had to be hospitalized for depression. Calvin, who blamed himself for the accident, did not admit to feeling depressed or discuss any of his feelings.

Shortly after the funeral, Calvin began to travel almost constantly. He couldn't stay at his office. He didn't feel comfortable at home. He traveled all over the world, sometimes purely for pleasure. He began to buy expensive things—an airplane and sports cars. However, the thrill of the new item would soon wear off, and he would then buy something else.

There were many aspects of running the business that Calvin avoided. The entire company was suffering significantly —all because the president was, without knowing it, self-treating his depression through excessive change.

Through some rather brief counseling, we showed Calvin what he was doing and why he was doing it. We told him that he was avoiding going through the proper grieving process and then helped him to fully admit his feelings of loss, to confront his self-blame (which was unfounded), and to be thankful for what he did have and continued to have. His performance returned to normal a few weeks after the counseling.

Causes of High Desire for Change

Change-oriented character develops in a very dynamic environment where change and creativity were emphasized, modeled, required, and rewarded. Routine ways may have been discouraged or at least not encouraged.

Very high desire for change can be a method of avoiding feelings of depression or anxiety, where change adds excitement and enjoyment. In this situation, change is used much as alcohol is often used to block out sad or nervous feelings.

■ Recognizing Desire for Change

Ask the person to tell you about several tasks she is responsible for doing over and over again, in much the same way, such as cutting the grass. For each task, ask: "How often do you do this?" "How much do you like doing this over and over?"

If the person is routine-oriented, you may find that she does routine tasks very regularly (as often as they really should be done) and that she either likes the tasks or doesn't mind doing them. If she is change-oriented, you may find that she puts off doing routine tasks or does them irregularly. You also may find that she does not like to do routine work and feels that it's boring.

Also ask: "Are there things you do that could be done in different ways?" "Do you change how you do these things?" "How would you feel about doing this differently each time?" "How would you feel about doing this the same way each time?"

If she is routine-oriented, you may find that she tends to do tasks the same way each time even when the tasks could be done in different ways. If she is change-oriented, she will change how she does the task from time to time.

It is possible that routine people may dress in clothes of an older style that they became accustomed to. If you see them on more than one occasion, you may find that they dress much the same. They may wear their hair in an old-fashioned style. Change-oriented people may choose new styles for their clothes and hair and change them frequently.

Observing dress and style is not really a very reliable way of measuring desire for change. For example, a person's spouse may buy his clothes for him. People often dress like others to conform to social pressures. A person may go back to an old style in an effort to be different from others in the present. Some people who would like to change more may not be able to afford to buy new things as frequently as styles change.

You can also ask other people, including references, about how they handle repetitive work. Have they been willing to make changes in their behavior and accept changes in their environment? Or have they made impractical changes?

■ Solutions to Problems

Desire for Change and Jobs

Routine people are very necessary to the operation of our society. Most jobs are more routine than not. Jobs such as working on a production line, cleaning and maintenance of buildings or equipment, teaching school, technologist or technician positions, cashier work, and many others require routine people.

However, change-oriented people are the ones who are largely responsible for the improvements and developments in fields such as medicine, electronics, manufacturing, architecture, government, and more.

Thomas Edison, who invented the light bulb, was undoubtedly a change-oriented person. So were Orville and Wilbur Wright, who made significant advances in the development of the airplane. The founding fathers of our country were definitely change-oriented.

Desire for Change and Relationships

Routine people normally feel more comfortable around and have fewer conflicts with other routine people—especially if they happen to enjoy the same routines. Similarly, change-oriented people normally feel more comfortable around and have fewer conflicts with other change-oriented people.

A routine person may be very attracted to a change-oriented person because the change-oriented person is exciting and imaginative. A change-oriented person may initially respect the consistency, stability, and dependability of the routine person. However, over time routine and change-oriented people can develop conflicts.

Routine people may be viewed as boring or rigid by highly change-oriented people. They may be threatened by the changes the change-oriented person wants to make. Change-oriented people may be viewed as impractical by routine people. They may feel stifled or confined by the sameness the routine person wants to maintain. The routine person may want to do things the old way while the change-oriented person wants to do things the new and improved way.

These incompatibilities can be successfully handled in any of three ways:

1) The routine person can become more change-oriented.
2) The change-oriented person can become more practical.
3) The two people can learn to appreciate the value of one being routine and the other change-oriented. They can also respect and appreciate one another's unique qualities.

Making the Routine Person Comfortable

To best relate to routine people, to make them comfortable, and to reduce conflict, let them:

- Have standard operating procedures.
- Do things the same way each time.
- Keep sameness or consistency in whom they know, where they are, what they have, when they do things, in their attitudes or beliefs, and in how they do things.
- Communicate respect for their routines and for what they are familiar with.

- Tell them about routines that you value and follow that are similar to their routines.
- If possible, don't pressure them to make significant changes or bother them with new ideas.
- Give them time to prepare before making necessary changes.
- Let others make or adjust to necessary changes.
- Let others help prepare them for necessary changes and reassure them throughout the process.
- Put them around other routine people.

Making the Change-oriented Person Comfortable

To best relate to change-oriented people, to make them comfortable, and to reduce conflict, let them:

- Do things in different ways each time.
- Change whom they know, where they are, what they have, when they do things, their attitudes or beliefs, and how they do things.
- Share and implement their new ideas.
- Make changes that are reasonably practical.
- Communicate respect for the changes they make and for what they find new and interesting.
- Tell them about what is new to you, especially if it is about something they are interested in.
- Don't pressure them to do much routine or repetitive work or bother them with how the old way was better.
- Let others do the more boring tasks.
- Put them around other change-oriented people.

Modifying the Routine Tendency

A friend or counselor could:

1) Listen to their opinion about what they think is wrong with changing something.
2) Restate what they have said so they will know the helper understands.
3) Be respectful of their opinion.
4) As much as they are willing, get them to consider the benefits of making the needed change and the consequences of not making the change.

Self-help for the Routine Person

- Learn to appreciate the value, feelings, and contributions of people with high desire for change.
- Keep a "change-oriented" log. Every day write down several ideas about what could be improved and consider the benefits of making the change.
- Recognize the limitations of sameness—lack of progress, not using methods that are proven to be more effective, lack of excitement, and settling for less.
- Confront your fears about what would happen if a change was made. See how you will be safe, important, and able to find happiness. See how you will successfully handle the change. Make an action plan that can be accomplished.
- Consider the advantages of a proposed change and the disadvantages of keeping things the same.
- Break out of ruts and try new things.
- Study the change to be made and make it in gradual, easy steps.

Modifying the Change-oriented Tendency

A friend or counselor could:
1) Listen to their opinion about what they think needs to be changed.
2) Restate what they have said so they will know the helper understands.
3) Be respectful of their opinion.
4) As much as they are willing, get them to consider potential problems, faults, and danger involved in the change.

Self-help for the Change-oriented Person

- Learn to appreciate the value of people who are more routine.
- If the change tendency is being used as a method of avoiding feelings of depression or anxiety, then the roots of the depression or anxiety should be discovered and discussed. Situations that trigger the depression or anxiety should be corrected.
- Be aware of what can be changed and what can't.
- Strongly and repetitively consider what is good about how things are and what is bad about a proposed change.
- Consider the value and necessity of specific routine tasks that must be done.
- Pair routine tasks with something you enjoy—for example, doing paperwork or cleaning while listening to music.
- Alternate routine work with nonroutine work to ward off boredom. Or routine work could be broken up into smaller parts and accomplished a little at a time.

Managing the Routine Person

Emphasize, model, require, and reward developing new behavior or new ideas. Consider discipline for lack of a desired new behavior or ideas and for doing what is more familiar but less desirable.

Managing the Change-oriented Person

Emphasize, model, require, and reward doing routine work. Consider discipline for lack of routine work and for making impractical change. Make the person aware of what is open for change and what is not. Get others to remind him or her to finish the routine work.

■ Get Your Pencil—Checkup Time

To Make This Information Useful to You, You Must Apply It!

1) Write down the type of person you fit best (routine or change-oriented).
2) Write down how being this way has helped and any specific problems it has caused.
3) If you have had problems with this area of emotional intelligence, then write down which solutions you will use to improve. Perhaps receive a desired reward for completing steps of your plan and for total completion.
4) Carry out the solutions you choose. Trying to change and repetition will make the action part of your character.

To Improve Relationships or to Help Others

1) Write down the type of person that someone you know fits best.
2) Write down how being this way has helped and any specific problems it has caused.
3) If that person has had problems with this area of emotional intelligence, then write down which solutions you will use to reduce conflict with him or her to build the person's performance. Perhaps he or she can receive a desired reward for completing steps of the plan and for total completion.
4) If you feel that the person is able and willing to receive this feedback, share your new insight with that person and tell him or her about what you think needs to be done.

Chapter 9

Measuring Courage

Courage is the willingness to risk injury, loss, hardship, or physical discomfort to reach a desired goal.

■ Low Courage—the Cautious Person

Clark is a librarian at a small branch library. Clark catalogs books and magazines and updates the card catalog so that people can find the books they want to read. When books are returned, Clark puts them back where they belong on the shelf. He works in a safe, comfortable environment. He's paid a moderate hourly wage plus insurance benefits. Clark seldom ventures to do things that are risky or challenging. He keeps all of his extra money in a savings account where he knows it's safe.

Strengths

The cautious person is one who scores low in courage. He or she plays it safe to avoid failure. Cautious people do what they can predict will turn out well, what is known to work, and what they are sure will work.

They are very safety-conscious and are good at staying out of dangerous situations. Cautious people can help to avoid losses, hardship, injury, and failure. Their motto is "It is better to be safe than sorry."

Being cautious is not the same as being careful. Careful people focus their attention and try to do things with precision. Cautious people simply avoid potentially negative circumstances. Someone may possess one, both, or neither of these qualities.

Here are some examples of how cautious people may behave in a given job setting:

A cautious person who is a purchasing agent may only buy familiar products from longtime suppliers. He or she wants to buy a tested product that works well.

A cautious person who is a bank executive wants to invest money in companies that are well known and sure to succeed. The bank earns moderate interest on these types of accounts and does not lose its money.

A cautious person who is a manager hires employees who have long-term, proven records of service. The manager typically would know the previous employer and trust the information he or she has received from that employer. As a result, new employees turn out to be good employees, just as expected.

Cautious people usually want safety and safety assurances. They want to know that there is little danger and that precautions have been taken. They want little chance of loss, injury, or hardship.

They desire an environment that is physically comfortable and free of unpleasant noise, excess temperature, or muscle strain.

Cautious people need assurances of job security with consistent income and benefits, including good insurance.

Potential Difficulties

Cautious people may give up too easily in the face of adversity and miss valuable opportunities. They may avoid risk and do what is safer but less valuable. They often let fear stop them from doing what they should do.

For example, the cautious purchasing agent mentioned above may not try out a new product or one with less documentation to prove its worth even though the new product may actually be twice as good as the old one and lower in price.

Cautious people may be too hesitant to act, resulting in slower achievement of difficult goals. A cautious entrepreneur may take ten years to build a business that a courageous entrepreneur might build in five years or less.

The performance of cautious people may suffer when they're in a crisis situation. In a crisis, cautious people are distracted by their fear, think less clearly, and lose coordination. In short, they choke under pressure. They do not enjoy participating in competition, since it often results in pressure, hardship, and loss.

Charles was thirty-five years old and lived at home with his mother. He had not held a job in ten years and was being supported by his father's money, which arrived once a month. During most of the day, he remained in a small but comfortable room.

Because of a fear of going outside, he saw little sunlight and was as white as a sheet. All of his muscles were seriously atrophied. When he stood up, his back slumped. When he was hungry, he would wait until no one was around, come out of his room, raid the refrigerator, and go back to his room. He was fearful of leaving his room, of meeting new people, and of failing at a job.

His mother initiated counseling for him. His first few counseling sessions had to be done over the phone. Then we visited him at his home where a major breakthrough involved Charles stepping out of his front door and walking around his block with his counselor. When Charles had overcome enough of his fears to be out in public again, we began to get him to consider going back to work. However, he was afraid that if he worked, his father would stop paying for his living expenses. He was afraid that he would get a job, lose his father's money, fail at the job, and have no income.

We were eventually able to encourage him to do volunteer work through some local churches. He got an apartment of his own and began to drive a car his father bought for him. When his car air conditioner failed, it was very important to Charles that it be fixed immediately so he would not get hot or sweat. When he later moved out of the city, he had other people move most of his things for him. He only moved a few light things that he could easily carry since he was afraid that he might strain a muscle.

Causes of Low Courage

Some children are simply born more cautious and fearful. Cautious children tend to explore less, stay away from things that hurt them, and give up more easily when they are trying to get something.

Low courage also may develop in an environment where fear of danger and the pursuit of safety were emphasized, modeled, required, and rewarded. Risk taking, competition, and determination may have been discouraged or at least not encouraged.

Low courage also may have developed as a result of experiencing harsh, frustrating situations or a feeling of failure. These people emerge with the determination to play it safe from now on.

■ High Courage—the Courageous Person

Craig is a United States Marine. He trains in combat maneuvers and does rigorous physical fitness exercises. In battle, he pushes his fear behind him and concentrates only on overcoming the adversary. When he is injured, he will keep fighting if possible, often enduring great physical pain.

Strengths
....

Courageous people will risk injury, loss, hardship, or personal failure to reach a desired goal. They enjoy challenging and unfamiliar tasks, excitement, and adventure. They enjoy winning and are highly competitive with others. They are often involved in physical forms of challenge or competition such as mountain climbing.

Courageous people are highly self-confident, believing that they can handle a variety of difficult circumstances. Courageous people think and work much harder when they're challenged by difficult circumstances. Even if they don't like hard work, they can work very hard when they are pursuing an important goal. They are very determined to reach their goals.

In the middle of a crisis, the courageous people are not distracted by fear. They usually don't "choke under pressure." In a crisis, they tend to focus only on what needs to be done to overcome the adversity. Adrenaline flows, thinking becomes more clear, and coordination improves.

Courageous people usually want the opportunity to advance in their careers. They also usually want to build their income according to their actual level of success. A courageous salesperson enjoys being paid by commission rather than by a safer yet more limiting hourly wage.

Potential Difficulties

Very courageous people try to prove their ability. They feel a need to win and may offend less competitive people. They tend to engage in win/lose contests that can annoy other people.

Very courageous people may overestimate their ability and do things before being well prepared. They tend to take large risks. In the pursuit of a good challenge, they may choose paths that cause loss, injury, or hardship.

Very courageous people are thrill seekers. To them, risk adds more fun. Some thrill seekers who are spontaneous are very dangerous to themselves and to others. A spontaneous thrill seeker who hang-glides may not get the best equipment, may not study the subject carefully, may not check the weather forecast, and may not carefully check his or her equipment before each flight.

Other thrill seekers who are careful may often be able to get the thrill and yet avoid loss, serious injury, etc. This would be true of hang gliders who buy top equipment, practice frequently, check the weather forecast, and inspect their equipment before each flight. Even with very good preparation, however, taking repeated risks eventually will result in a negative consequence for most people.

Harry Houdini, originally named Erik Weisz, was an American magician noted for his sensational and often dangerous escape acts. Houdini possessed great physical strength and agility. As a young man, he won many athletic honors. Later, he performed before crowds as a trapeze artist. In one of his escape acts, he was chained and placed in a box that was locked, roped, and weighted. The box was dropped from a boat and sank to the bottom of the bay. He managed to free himself and swim to the surface. In another act, he was suspended head down, about seventy-five feet above ground, and freed himself from a straitjacket.

Although many of his performances were life-threatening, Houdini was never seriously injured in one of them due to his unusual physical abilities and careful planning of each act. He was both careful and courageous. However, his death did eventually come as a result of a risk that he took. He publicly boasted that he could take a punch from anyone in his abdomen. One day a young man came up to him and, without giving Houdini time to tighten his abdominal muscles, hit him in the stomach. Houdini later died from peritonitis that stemmed from the stomach injury.

Causes of High Courage

Courage is present at birth for many people. Some children explore more, climb higher, and show less avoidance of things that have hurt or startled them. Others develop their courage later as a result of their experiences and environment.

Courage can develop in an environment where risk taking, competition, and determination were emphasized, modeled, required, and rewarded. Thoughts of danger and the pursuit of safety may have been discouraged or at least not encouraged.

Courage also may have developed as a result of experiencing a difficult environment where courage was necessary and caution or conservatism didn't meet basic needs. For example, Houdini's acts became progressively more dangerous in order to garner more attention and success.

■ Identifying the Cautious or Courageous Person

Ask someone to describe a crisis, a difficult obstacle, or an unpleasant circumstance in his life. Don't tell him what you are looking for. Just keep him talking about what happened and about how he felt. Listen carefully to discover how he handled the adversity.

If the person is cautious, you may find that he avoided the adversity or discomfort. He also may have performed more poorly because of fear. If he is courageous, he probably faced the challenge, increased his efforts, and strongly pursued his goal—despite hardship. An extremely courageous person may have taken excessive risks or did not give up when it made more sense to stop.

In a brief meeting, you probably can't tell by sight whether a person is courageous or not. Courage is most visible under fire when a person is actively dealing with adversity. It is out of the question in most interviewing settings to start a fire so you can observe how the person responds.

Most people who exercise vigorously are courageous to some degree, and in these people you may notice an athletic build. However, also be aware that not all courageous people vigorously exercise. Other people, including references, may be able to tell you about a person's response to crises, difficulty, and discomfort and about his risk-taking tendencies.

■ Solutions to Problems

Courage and Jobs

Cautious people are valuable to organizations and to society. They prevent major danger or loss from occurring. Typical examples are accountants, mathematicians, statisticians, secretaries, bookkeepers, pharmacists, personnel clerks, safety managers, and many others. Their safety orientation can help balance the tendencies of more courageous people.

Courageous people are also valuable to our society. Courage was necessary for early explorers to make discoveries, and it was necessary in fighting to gain control of our country. Courage continues to be necessary to run and manage our country.

Courage is a major factor in being an entrepreneur or a founder of an organization. Courage is necessary in salespeople who must open a new territory. Athletes, soldiers, and physical laborers must have courage to deal with physical pain and discomfort.

Courage and Relationships

Cautious people normally feel more comfortable around and have fewer conflicts with other cautious people. They tend to agree on maintaining safety and comfort. Courageous people also tend to agree with each other about facing challenges and tolerating discomfort in pursuing goals.

A cautious person may be attracted to a courageous person out of respect for his bravery and determination. The cautious person may feel safe if the courageous person will protect him. A courageous person may enjoy the admiration of the cautious person. However, there is a tendency over time for cautious and courageous people to develop conflicts.

Cautious people may be fearful of the chances high-courage people may take. Courageous people may disrespect low-courage people, feeling they are too fearful. Cautious people might suffer name-calling labels such as "wimp" or "baby" from people who are very courageous (or think they are) and who are critical.

These conflicts are solvable if any of three things happen:

1) The cautious person can become more courageous.

2) The courageous person can become more cautious.

3) The two people can learn to appreciate the value of one being cautious and the other courageous. They also can respect and appreciate one another's unique qualities.

Making the Cautious Person Comfortable

To best relate to a cautious person, to make that person comfortable, and to reduce conflict, give him:

- A setting that is safe and free from the chance of physical harm.
- A setting that is physically comfortable.
- Assurance that his financial and physical needs will always be met.

- Respect for his safety habits.
- Avoid putting him into competitive situations where he could lose or fail.
- Reassure that person when he is afraid.
- Let others handle situations that involve risk, discomfort, or potential loss.
- Let others respond to crises or face adverse situations.
- Put him around other cautious people.

Making the Courageous Person Comfortable

To best relate to a courageous person, to make her comfortable, and to reduce conflict, give her:
- Challenging circumstances and adventure.
- Pay according to her level of success.
- Respect for her bravery and determination.
- Let others handle parts of the job that are nonchallenging or that involve ensuring safety and preparation for hardship situations.
- Let others calculate risk and danger before taking major action.
- Put her around other courageous people.

Modifying the Cautious Tendency

A friend or counselor could:
1) Listen to that person's opinion about what he thinks is dangerous or unpleasant.
2) Restate what the cautious person said so he will know the helper understands.
3) Be respectful of his opinion.

4) As much as he is willing, get that person to consider the excitement and opportunity involved in a challenging situation.

Self-help for the Cautious Person

- Learn to appreciate the value, feelings, and contributions of people with high courage.
- Keep a "courage" log. Each day, spend at least ten minutes considering things that you avoid doing because of fear or that you have trouble doing because of fear. Write down how you can successfully handle each part of the task and what is good about doing the task. Visualize yourself succeeding and the rewards of completing the task.
- When you are in a crisis situation, focus 100 percent of your attention on what you need to do to complete the task. Totally push out other thoughts like "What if I fail?" "I might get hurt," or "I can't do this." Think, "I will successfully handle this by … "
- Look at challenging situations as valuable opportunities to learn, improve, benefit, and enjoy. Take calculated risks.
- Gradually face more discomfort, hardship, and pressure. Getting on an exercise program can build some courage. Check with your doctor first.
- Get others to communicate their confidence in your ability to succeed and to overcome.

Modifying the Courageous Tendency

A friend or counselor could:

1) Listen to her opinion about what she thinks is good about taking a risk or facing adversity.

2) Restate what she has said so that person will know the helper understands.

3) Be respectful of her opinion.

4) As much as she is willing, get that person to consider potential problems, risks, or danger involved.

Self-help for the Courageous Person

- Learn to appreciate the value and contributions of people who are cautious.
- Deal with compulsive ideas such as "I will never give up" or "I have to prove that I'm not a wimp by doing something dangerous." Examine the basis for the compulsion to take risks. Learn to value yourself when others win.
- Learn the acceptability and value of safety and caution.
- Keep a "cautious" attitude log. Each day, spend at least ten minutes considering what you have done or might do that is unnecessarily dangerous. Write down what is negative, wrong, or dangerous about doing the task. Visualize yourself experiencing negative consequences because of taking excess risk.
- Check plans for excessive risk or danger. Learn when to give up.
- Calculate risks, danger, and your ability before acting. Risk only as is necessary. Risk only what you can afford to lose.

Managing the Cautious Person

Emphasize, model, require, and reward taking risks, competition, facing difficulty, and determination. Consider discipline for lack of courageous behavior.

Managing the Courageous Person
....

Emphasize, model, require, and reward safety and caution. Consider discipline for taking excessive risk.

■ Get Your Pencil—Checkup Time

To Make This Information Useful to You, You Must Apply It!

1) Write down the type of person you fit best (cautious or courageous).
2) Write down how being this way has helped and any specific problems it has caused.
3) If you have had problems with this area of emotional intelligence, then write down which solutions you will use to improve. Perhaps receive a desired reward for completing steps of your plan and for total completion.
4) Carry out the solutions you choose. Trying to change and repetition will make the action part of your character.

To Improve Relationships or to Help Others

1) Write down the type of person that someone you know fits best.
2) Write down how being this way has helped and any specific problems it has caused.
3) If that person has had problems with this area of emotional intelligence, then write down which solutions you will use to reduce conflict with that person or to build his or her performance. Perhaps that person can receive a desired reward for completing steps of the plan and for total completion.
4) If you feel that the person is able and willing to receive this feedback, share your new insight with that person and tell him or her about what you think needs to be done.

Chapter 10

Measuring
Self-direction

S elf-direction is the tendency to form opinions, set goals, and make decisions.

■ Low Self-direction—the Hesitant Person

Helen is a general office secretary. She does light bookkeeping, answers the phone, types letters from a Dictaphone, opens and distributes the mail, mails out correspondence written by her boss, buys a few office supplies, and files projects and records. All of her duties are structured. She is rarely called upon to make creative decisions.

Every day she does what she has been trained to do. Her training comes from both a business-skills school she attended and from several years of job experience. When anything unusual comes up, Helen asks her boss what he wants to do. She's very indecisive, but it doesn't hurt her in this job. Her indecisiveness makes her more willing to follow the direction of others, which suits her boss's personality very well.

Strengths

The hesitant person scores low in self-direction. Hesitant people value support and guidance from others and like to follow procedures set by others. They feel more secure when they have job structure. They want others to make major decisions, set goals, make plans, and prioritize.

When hesitant people make decisions, they want plenty of time so that they can avoid making the wrong decision. If hesitant people are also assertive, they can tell others what to do but still feel the need for much direction from their leader.

Hesitancy is appropriate in many worker-level jobs since many workers are expected to simply follow their leaders' directions. Hesitancy also can be appropriate in some lower-level management positions where the manager is largely responsible for getting a group of workers to do work in a way that has been determined by others above the manager.

Potential Difficulties

Hesitant people have difficulty setting goals, making plans, prioritizing, and initiating action. They are more dependent on others and their ideas and may make decisions too slowly in some settings. Solutions to problems are often delayed or missed. Problems then may persist and worsen.

Hesitant people are often unsure of the decisions they *do* make. After making a decision, they may doubt it and change their minds. Indecisiveness also limits creativity. A person who has a great idea may not be able to decide what to do with it without adequate decisiveness.

Hesitancy is generally more of a problem for people who are in executive positions since executives usually must make major decisions for an organization.

When they're together in a group, hesitant people get frustrated with each other because of lack of leadership. The following is a typical conversation between two hesitant people in an unstructured situation:

Person 1 "What do you want to do?"

Person 2 "I don't know. What do you want to do?"

Person 1 "I don't know. I'd like to know what you want to do."

Hilda was one of the most indecisive people I have ever known in all my years of counseling. She went to college because her parents expected her to go. In college, Hilda couldn't decide on a major and finally dropped out because her money ran out. After college, Hilda couldn't decide which job to apply for. She needed career counseling to help her determine what she should be doing.

Once it was determined that sales was her best job possibility, she needed much help in deciding whom to call on, how to get an interview, and even what to say in an interview. When she got more than one job offer, she couldn't decide which one she wanted the most. Without help, she probably would have hesitated until the offers evaporated.

After she was helped to pick which job to accept, she had constant questions about how to relate to others on the job, especially her manager. On the job, she was slow to make sales contacts because she couldn't decide who would be good to call on. She even had trouble deciding which routes to take to make calls. When she did call on a customer, she had difficulty helping the customer decide which of her many products the customer should buy.

Hilda also had trouble determining whom to date and for how long, what to do on a date, how to deal with dating problems, whether to repair her car and how, where to live, how much to pay for an apartment, which city to live in, whether a pain was serious enough to see a doctor, which doctor to see, what to do about a traffic accident, which church she should go to on Sunday, how to move her furniture to the next apartment, and how to relate to a sister who belittled her. In every aspect of her life, Hilda had trouble making decisions.

These are only a fraction of the decisions that were brought up over a three-year period of counseling. Hilda's main problem was not intelligence but rather a strong fear of making the wrong decision. We dealt with Hilda's fears as is described later in the "Solutions to Problems" section of this chapter. After three years of building her emotional intelligence in this area, Hilda was able to make almost all of her decisions on her own. She then only sought help from others when she needed information or technical data important to making her own decision.

Causes of Low Self-direction

Low self-direction can develop in an environment where following written or spoken instructions was emphasized, modeled, required, and rewarded. Independent decision making may have been discouraged or at least not encouraged.

Low self-direction also may develop as a result of depression. In this situation, the person feels a sense of helplessness that his or her "decisions won't do any good, anyway." The person may be tired or burned out. Decision making may seem to take too much effort.

Finally, a person may become indecisive because of excessive fear of making the wrong decisions. This fearfulness could actually stem from being faultfinding and from being low in courage.

■ High Self-direction—the Decisive Person

Dan is the top executive of a large company he built from the ground up. He had made good money as vice president of operations of a major hotel chain but progressively wanted to do things his own way. Eventually he struck out on his own once he felt he had the necessary skills and knowledge. Dan invested his own money, interested some other investors, and bought a hotel to run. After making a considerable profit, he bought more hotels, most of which became very profitable. With each hotel, he changed policy, procedure, and personnel. He also solved problems such as how to attract more customers and how to cut costs.

Strengths

The decisive person is one who is high in self-direction. Decisive people have confidence in their own ideas and can make decisions quickly. They can look at a situation and confidently form opinions, drawing their own conclusions. They set goals for themselves, determine their own priorities, and initiate action. They are resourceful.

Decisive people like some freedom from control, less supervision, power, authority, and independence. They want to find their own solutions to problems and don't like merely following the structure or procedures that others have set.

Those who are moderate to high in self-direction are willing to let others participate in the decision-making process.

Decisive people shape the environment around them. Once aware of problems, they boldly plan ways of solving them. An architect, for example, decides how a building will look and how to make it safe. An interior designer decides how a room will look, feel, and function.

If they are also assertive, decisive people may get others involved in completing the plan. These assertive and decisive people become our top leaders, both in business and in government. Every president our country has had fits this emotional intelligence mold.

Potential Difficulties
....

Being strongly self-directed is not a problem in and of itself. However, when decisive people have jobs that don't allow them to make decisions, they feel limited and frustrated. In this situation, they may resist support, guidance, and procedures—and may try to control decisions more than they should.

If people are extremely high in self-direction, they are autocratic. They tend to reject the guidance of most other people and try to control virtually all decisions affecting them. They may get into power struggles with other people who are high to very high in self-direction. Their motto is "my way or the highway."

Duke is excessively controlling. He determines the direction of every major project his company works on. His executives must report to him and give him information so that he can make all decisions. He has little patience with anyone who disagrees with him. Several of his good executives who were strong leaders have quit because they didn't like being under his thumb all the time.

The company is 100 percent Duke's company. He didn't set up a board of directors because he didn't want to answer to anyone. He also has no business partner.

There are many customers who have stopped doing business with Duke because he was too controlling. He was too arbitrary about how much his customers should pay for his service and tried to determine which product customers should use despite their wishes. He also tried to control how the customer would use the product once it was bought. The few customers he has left are the ones who are willing to be dominated or those who have not yet had enough of his controlling tactics.

At home, he is an absolute monarch. He might as well wear a purple robe, a golden crown, and sit on a throne in the living room. His wife and children do just as he asks. Because his wife is extremely dependent and not very assertive, she argues with him very little. However, she feels emotionally battered and beaten. Whatever Duke wants, he gets.

Duke tightly controls the money. Even though they have plenty of money, if his wife wants to buy anything but groceries and gas for her car, she has to ask Duke's permission. Her self-esteem has suffered a great deal from this relationship. She has also come to doubt her own ability to make decisions and to solve problems.

Duke is also very assertive. Without assertiveness, he would have found ways to control that were more manipulative and not as direct.

Causes of High Self-direction

High self-direction develops in an environment where independent decision making was emphasized, modeled, required, and rewarded. Following written or spoken instructions may have been discouraged or at least not encouraged.

High self-direction may have developed as a result of being in an environment where a person was hurt emotionally or physically. He or she may have decided that to avoid being hurt again, being in control is necessary.

Finally, there is a genetic predisposition to being decisive or indecisive. Some children are simply born more decisive, more confident, more active, and more aggressive than others.

Identifying Self-direction

Ask someone to describe several significant problems or unpleasant circumstances that happened to him. Don't tell him what you are looking for. Just keep him talking about what happened and about how he felt. Listen carefully to discover if he decided what to do, how quickly he decided, and how he decided upon what to do.

If he is hesitant, you may find that he avoided making a decision, took a very long time to make it, or looked to someone else to make the decision. If people are decisive, they probably faced the problem—and rather quickly—decided on how to solve the problem. They may have made the decision themselves, or they may have sought the opinions of others before making the decision. An extremely decisive person will control the decision and give no control to others.

In an interview, you could set up job-related problems and ask the candidate to tell you what he would do if these situations came up. Again, let him bear the burden for explaining just what he would do.

Other people, including references, may be able to tell you about the person's willingness to work within structure set by others, if that person made decisions, how he or she made decisions, and the effectiveness of those decisions.

■ Solutions to Problems

Self-direction and Jobs

Hesitant people usually don't make quick, rash, or impulsive decisions. They feel the need for guidance from others and, therefore, tend to become followers. Followers are necessary to all organizations, especially as various laborers, office workers, and technicians. Even some salespeople have a very structured role to play where hesitation will not hurt their performance.

Decisiveness is a quality that is necessary for success in jobs such as analyst, practitioner, product developer, engineer, scientist, business executive, and in sales jobs that involve problem solving.

Self-direction and Relationships

Hesitant people can be very comfortable with other hesitant people *if* they are members of a group that is lead by a decisive yet considerate person. This relationship is roughly like that of a group of sheep to their benevolent shepherd. Yet, without the benevolent shepherd, these people may feel very insecure together.

Hesitant people feel the need for capable leadership. They need to have confidence in their leader. Their leader should know what to do and clearly communicate it. Hesitant people are most comfortable with those who are both decisive and considerate of their needs.

Hesitant people seek out relationships with people who will make decisions with or for them. In a marriage, for instance, where someone should make decisions to meet the daily needs of the pair, hesitant people actually seem to be least compatible with other hesitant people. In this relationship, both wonder what to do, neither is able to solve major problems, and both tend to feel insecure as a result.

A hesitant person may be attracted to an extremely decisive person out of respect for their sense of direction and ability to solve problems. While he or she may later feel controlled by the extremely decisive person, the hesitant person may still like this relationship if the extremely decisive person is very thoughtful of their needs. Both decisive and extremely decisive people may be attracted to more hesitant people because they can clearly determine how things will happen in this relationship.

Decisive people usually get along well with people who are nondecisive. However, if a decisive person is in a management or executive position and supervises a person who is also in a management or executive position, the decisive boss may expect the subordinates to pull their share of the load and to make decisions in their area of responsibility. In this situation, the hesitant executive or manager will be viewed by the decisive boss as being weak or ineffective.

Decisive people tend to get along well with other decisive people and are best managed by leaders who are also decisive. Hesitant and normally decisive people are compatible with decisive people as followers, but decisive people are hard to manage for hesitant people.

A decisive person may enjoy being led by an extremely decisive person if the leader is able and is considerate of that person; if the leader has other decisions to keep him or her busy; and if the leader is not a perfectionist with a tendency to micromanage and control all decisions at the decisive person's level of responsibility. Otherwise, there is likely to be a power struggle.

Extremely decisive people tend to get into power struggles with other extremely decisive people, especially when leadership roles have not been clearly communicated and agreed upon. If they are not assertive, these power struggles may be more covert than overt.

Making the Hesitant Person Comfortable

To best relate to hesitant people, to make them comfortable, and to reduce conflict, give them:

- Procedures.
- Specific guidance.
- A plan to follow.
- Help in making decisions.
- Much time to make decisions.
- Confirmation of their decision if they make one.
- Clear-cut priorities.

- Respect and appreciation for following other's guidance.
- Let others make decisions with or for them.
- Put them with a benevolent and capable leader.

Making the Decisive Person Comfortable

To best relate to decisive people, to make them comfortable, and to reduce conflict, let them:
- Form opinions.
- Make decisions.
- Solve problems.
- Set goals.
- Determine priorities.
- Receive respect for their decisions.
- Have some freedom from procedures and others' control.
- Put them around other people who are moderate to high in self-direction.
- If practical, and if they are competent, give them a higher level of authority and responsibility where they can make decisions.
- Give *extremely* self-directed people absolute control and praise for their decisions.
- Let others follow orders and procedures.
- Put them around people who are dependent and nonassertive enough to be dominated.

Modifying the Hesitant Tendency

A friend or counselor could:
1) Listen to their opinion about a problem they can't decide how to solve.

2) Restate what they have said so that they will know the helper understands.

3) Be respectful of their plight.

4) Help them to identify the problem, generate options, weigh pros and cons, make the decision, plan steps, and take action.

Self-help for the Hesitant Person

- Learn to appreciate the value, feelings, and contributions of people with higher self-direction.

- Keep a "self-direction" log. Each day, spend at least ten minutes considering problems that need to be solved. Identify the problem, generate options, weigh pros and cons, make the decision, plan steps, and take action. Visualize yourself succeeding and the rewards of completing the task.

- If low self-direction is caused by depression, then the root causes and situations that trigger the depression should be discovered and corrected. If caused by poor health or stress, these causes must be corrected.

- Be more decisive. This would involve identifying problems, generating options, weighing pros and cons, making decisions, planning steps, and acting faster.

Modifying the Excessively Decisive Tendency

A friend or counselor could:

1) Listen to their opinion about what they think is good about a solution or a decision they have made.

2) Restate what they have said so they will know the helper understands.

3) Be respectful of their opinion.

4) As much as they are willing, get them to consider potential problems involved or to consider the value of including others in the decision.

Self-help for the Excessively Decisive Person

• Learn to appreciate the value of people who are hesitant.

• Deal with compulsive ideas such as "I must be in control." Examine the basis for the compulsion to control decisions.

• Learn the acceptability and value of following others and of making team decisions.

• Keep a "following" log. Each day, spend at least ten minutes considering how you should be following the direction of others or should be sharing decisions. Write down what is good, right, and reasonable about doing this. Visualize yourself following or sharing decisions, experiencing positive consequences.

• Consider whether letting someone else make the decision prevents you from meeting your emotional and physical needs. If not, then you don't need to make the decision, although you might want to.

• Learn to value others' ideas and opinions and to discriminate between competent, trustworthy people and incompetent, untrustworthy people. Learn to trust the decisions of competent people, and let others participate in or make decisions.

Managing the Hesitant Person

Emphasize, model, require, and reward setting goals, making decisions, solving problems, and planning. Consider discipline for lack of decisive behavior.

Managing the Excessively Decisive Person

Emphasize, model, require, and reward following others or sharing decisions. Consider discipline for taking control of tasks, especially those that are not a part of their responsibility. If a power struggle occurs, tell them they can decide, but point out the consequences.

■ Get Your Pencil—Check-up Time

To Make This Information Useful to You, You Must Apply It!

1) Write down the type of person you fit best (hesitant or decisive).
2) Write down how being this way has helped and any specific problems it has caused.
3) If you have had problems with this area of emotional intelligence, then write down which solutions you will use to improve. Perhaps receive a desired reward for completing steps of your plan and for total completion.
4) Carry out the solutions you choose. Trying to change and repetition will make the action part of your character.

To Improve Relationships or to Help Others

1) Write down the type of person that someone you know fits best.
2) Write down how being this way has helped and any specific problems it has caused.
3) If that person has had problems with this area of emotional intelligence, then write down which solutions you will use to reduce conflict with him or her or to build that person's performance. Perhaps he or she can receive a desired reward for completing steps of the plan and for total completion.
4) If you feel that the person is able and willing to receive this feedback, share your new insight with that person and tell him or her about what you think needs to be done.

Chapter 11

Measuring Assertiveness

Assertiveness measures to what degree a person tries to motivate others to believe or do something. It also measures to what degree a person resists complying with others.

■ Low Assertiveness—the Compliant Person

Carl is a chemist who works for a chemical company in a laboratory creating formulas for products such as insecticides. The formulas are then used by plant supervisors and workers in the daily production of the chemical. Carl's boss provides him with whatever he needs to succeed, including special equipment. Carl concentrates on his own work, has no management duties, and maintains a relatively low profile. However, he is one of the highest-paid employees in the plant.

Strengths
....

Compliant people usually listen and cooperate. They tend to be agreeable and tactful. They're not argumentative or overly critical and are submissive and conforming, particularly to those in authority. Compliant people give others the opportunity to express themselves and do as they wish. They are not pushy, forceful, dominating, or overbearing.

Compliant people prefer doing their own work or being a member of a team that is lead by someone else. They want to be in a setting with little conflict or hostility, where they feel accepted.

Potential Difficulties

Compliant people find it difficult to be assertive with others. It's hard for them to get their opinion across. They aren't persuasive. It's difficult for them to stick up for their point of view in a discussion or in an argument, so they have difficulty selling products or services unless these products or services are already in high demand. They are not closers. In management situations, they have trouble motivating employees.

Compliant people have difficulty getting compliance from others, and they quickly yield to the demands of others. They have trouble saying "no," tend to be pushed around by others, and easily give up their wants and needs. They may say or do what they think others expect and tend to avoid saying or doing what others may dislike.

They have a low tendency to require, insist on, or demand what they want from others. If the compliant person is in a position of leadership and if his or her employees are demanding, the leader will have little control. Compliance inhibits delegating responsibility to others and makes discipline a problem.

Compliant people may be intimidated by other people who readily engage in conflict. Their performance is disturbed when they are exposed to arguments or heated discussions. As a result, they may not engage in enough conflict to solve a problem.

Connie is a single mother of three boys. Her husband left the family when the boys were very young. As the children grew up, they became progressively more demanding, and Connie gave in to their demands. When they were younger, they would often turn down the food she made them and get her to fix something else. She had trouble getting them to go to bed on time and to stop watching television. If they didn't want to take a bath, they didn't take a bath. As bad as this was, it was just the beginning.

When the boys were nine to thirteen years old, they would argue with Connie until she gave them money. They stayed out late, didn't do homework, started smoking cigarettes, drinking alcohol, and using foul language. The boys not only began to steal merchandise from stores, they also took Connie's money without her knowing it. They did no household chores and destroyed the house during fights with each other. As you would walk through the house, you would see holes in the wall, broken plates, food stains on furniture, and papers and clothing strewn everywhere.

Connie would threaten to punish the boys but rarely followed through. When they would misbehave, she was indirect about telling them to stop, sometimes making a joke out of her request. She would timidly ask them to stop at least three times before they would even act like they heard her. She would try to explain to them why they should do something and would even beg them to behave. If she was going to come into the house with a date, she would pay them or otherwise bribe them to keep the house clean and to act nice while her date was there.

Causes of Low Assertiveness

Some children are naturally more passive and nonassertive. Parents of these children find them easy to manage. They like to please and easily sit through meals, pick up their toys, and go to bed when asked.

Compliance also develops in environments where listening, cooperating, and submitting were emphasized, modeled, required, and rewarded. Persuading, making demands, or open disagreement may have been discouraged or punished. Sometimes in trying to make model children who quietly obey like robots, parents inhibit assertiveness.

If a child is criticized, rejected, or physically or verbally punished for expressing opinions, the child is unlikely to develop assertiveness.

■ High Assertiveness—the Assertive Person

Alice is a hospital floor nurse. Her duties involve seeing that each patient takes the medication that the doctor has prescribed. She cleans wounds, replaces bandages, moves patients in their beds, makes sure they are ready to go to surgery, and takes vital signs.

She makes sure the patient eats only the food that the hospital nutritionist has sent. If she sees a patient with a candy bar or an alcoholic beverage, she must pleasantly but assertively take it from him or her. Often she has to wake a patient in the middle of the night to give medicine. Regularly patients will resist her efforts.

If a patient isn't doing as well as expected, Alice calls the doctor to let him or her know what she thinks is happening. Sometimes she has to tell the doctor that he or she is doing something wrong with the patient.

Alice enforces visiting hours and asks people who aren't supposed to be there, such as solicitors, to leave the hospital. If there's a mess in a room, she calls the cleaning crew. If two patients are in a double room and one patient has the television turned up too loud, Alice settles the dispute. Sometimes patients try to leave before their treatment is complete or before they have paid, and Alice must intervene.

Strengths

Assertive people are comfortable expressing their opinions or beliefs despite lack of approval from others. They easily express what they like and dislike. They are convincing when sharing their ideas and can often influence others' thoughts and actions.

They are comfortable requiring, insisting on, and demanding what they want. They tell others what they want, need, or expect. They are also comfortable telling others what to do and what not to do. Assertive people comfortably give orders. They tend to be able to maintain control over those they manage.

Assertive people can comfortably disagree with others, argue when necessary, and say no. They can face and deal with interpersonal conflict and can confront others. They do not usually feel the need to conform or please others. Assertive people are willing to punish or apply consequences if others don't comply with their demands.

Here are some examples of how assertive people might express themselves: "I want six copies by 5 P.M.," "Please put these boxes over there," "Sir, you must stop smoking in this nonsmoking area," and "If you don't stop coming in late for work, we will have to find someone else to do your job!"

Assertive people like being in charge. They like directing people and giving instructions. Assertive people want some power and authority, so they enjoy leadership positions—usually in sales or management.

Assertiveness in sales involves getting an appointment despite resistance, going over all of the sales material with the prospect, asking for the business, and not lowering the selling price too much or giving away products or services without proper payment.

It should be noted that assertiveness should be done at a level and manner appropriate to the situation. Also, other qualities like sociability can help make the demand more acceptable. Even though the assertive person is able to lead others, they also can be lead and managed by those in authority. They have the ability to cooperate with others.

Potential Difficulties

Assertive people have a need to be assertive. If an assertive person is not in a position of leadership, he or she will be frustrated and may try to find ways of leading, even if it's not part of the job structure.

Extremely assertive people are compelled to be assertive. They can be pushy, impatient, and forceful about getting what they want. They may forcefully and frequently express their opinions or beliefs and won't rest until others agree with them. They require, insist on, and demand what they want from others in an overbearing manner. They try to dominate others and are generally argumentative. Winning an argument may become more important to them than trying to decide who is right. They readily engage in interpersonal conflict and can be blunt or too frank in their confrontation of others. Extremely assertive people tend to be very ready to punish others for noncompliance and may be too severe in doing it. The dictators of the world have all been extremely assertive.

Here are some examples of how extremely assertive people express themselves: "Our product is better than all of the others. You need to order at least three cases today. I'll just fill out this order form for you," "Make me six copies—pronto!" "Stop smoking in this nonsmoking area or leave!" and "You were late to work! You're fired! Pack your things and get out!"

Extremely assertive people feel the need to be in charge and in control. They need power and authority and enjoy top leadership positions—usually in sales or management. They may try to direct situations they have not been given authority to control. The extremely assertive person is uncooperative, not submissive, and very difficult to manage.

Many years ago, I was with some friends at a church dinner and began to talk about how the nursery and children's area of the church was in need of repair. Those of us who were assertive worked together and came to a group decision to meet on Saturday morning with our tools and supplies to make improvements.

On Saturday morning, we had been working on the rooms for nearly an hour when Alex burst into the room. He had heard that we were doing renovation work and had come to help. He almost instantly began to tell everyone else what to do, as if they were not already doing what should be done, and as if he was the leader of the entire project. Virtually every word out of his mouth was a command or an order. I seriously doubt that General Patton was ever any more assertive than Alex was.

Besides the fact that most of us didn't like being pushed around or yelled at, the worst problem was that Alex didn't know how to paint, how to wallpaper, or how to lay new carpet. Because he was also excessively self-directed, he didn't draw from the skills of the group. Instead, he made autocratic, unilateral decisions.

He began directing most of us to do the wrong things. For example, we were being instructed to put the new carpet in before the room was painted. Following his instructions, the carpet was being laid in such a way that there were wavy spots and creases in it. Some who were more skilled at painting were told to carry out trash, while people who had never painted before were told to paint.

Alex is a sales representative for a company that sells photocopiers. Six days a week, Alex walks though the business areas of town and tries to meet the owners or purchasing agents of each business. His tactics are very aggressive. He'll find where the key decision maker is located in the building and then try to get the secretary to let him see the boss.

First, he must sell the secretary on the idea of letting him see the person in charge. When he talks to the prospect, he presents his product as being the best possible equipment.

He goes off into a monologue about the features and benefits of the copier then asks the prospect what his or her objections would be to buying the machine.

As soon as an objection is mentioned, Alex shoots it down with his own reasoning. If the prospect isn't interested, this only means to Alex that he hasn't tried the right angle yet. If people say they don't have time right now, Alex says he'll only take another minute and talks about how much time the machine will save them. If they say it costs too much, he compares the price to other more expensive copiers and shows them how the copier will save money. If the prospect has another copier, he looks up the copier in his copier book and tells the prospect why *his* copier is better. He then offers to take the old copier as part of a trade. Alex will offer the customer a special low price if the customer buys now. He says he can't offer this low price at a later date.

You almost have to throw Alex out of the office to get rid of him. Many customers allow themselves to be dominated by Alex and buy his products. To his credit, Alex does get to talk to many customers whom other less assertive salespeople never see. However, there are also many people who become offended by the pressure he uses and tell him to never come back. They may later buy from another salesperson who shows more respect for their right to choose.

Causes of High Assertiveness

Some children are born to be more assertive than others. Even as infants and toddlers, you can see them demanding to be fed, picked up, or given a toy they see.

Assertiveness also may develop in an environment where being assertive was allowed, emphasized, modeled, required, and rewarded. Being compliant may have been discouraged or punished.

Assertiveness also develops in an environment where assertiveness was necessary to meet physical or emotional needs. For instance, a person who is given a management position may have to become assertive to keep his or her job.

■ Identifying Assertiveness

If you are interviewing a person for a job, ask her to tell you why she should get this job.

The compliant person may quietly and timidly tell you why she should get the job. The assertive person will strongly assert to you reasons why she should get the job. The extremely assertive person will dominate the conversation and pressure you. You may be sorry you asked her the question.

Get her to tell you about a time when she saw something that was significant to her one way and someone else saw it another way. Again let her carry the conversation while you listen for timidity or assertiveness.

You can also ask her to give you an example of when she was in a group that had to take some sort of action. In an unstructured group setting, compliant people tend to wait for others to take control. Assertive people will open channels of communication and discuss their opinions of what should be done. Extremely assertive people often immediately assume they are the leader and begin to direct everyone. This works out if they really know what the group should do or if they are low enough in self-direction to be willing to include other members of the group in decision making.

Assertiveness is one of the easier characteristics to notice by observation. However, realize that extremely assertive people may be watching their manners to impress you, and compliant people may psyche themselves up to be more assertive for a short meeting with you.

Other people, including references, should be able to tell you how the person expressed opinions, handled disagreements, gave instructions to others, faced conflict, got cooperation from others, cooperated with others, and submitted to her boss.

■ Solutions to Problems

Assertiveness and Jobs

Compliant people are generally easy to get along with and easy to lead. Being compliant is one of the major characteristics that causes a person to be a follower instead of being a leader—a doer instead of a delegator. Since there are numerous jobs that call for compliant people, being compliant can be a successful lifestyle. Examples include various laborers, office workers, some accountants, and technicians.

However, being compliant can be a problem in sales, in management, and in other circumstances where strong verbal assertion is necessary.

Assertive people are the authority figures in our society. They sell, manage, and enforce. Assertiveness is a key element to the success of any leader. However, the type of demand and the force behind the demand must always be appropriate to the setting. This requires some judgment and often some consideration for others' needs. Assertiveness is also seldom used all by itself in relating to others. It usually must be used along with other important qualities such as sociability and consideration for others.

Assertiveness and Relationships

Compliant people can be very comfortable with other compliant people if they are members of a group that is lead by an assertive, yet considerate person. This relationship is roughly like that of a group of children to its sweet but assertive nursery school teacher. Without the teacher, the children may feel very insecure.

Compliant people feel the need for people who will be assertive for them. In a marriage where someone must be assertive to meet the daily needs of the couple, compliant people actually seem to be least compatible with other compliant people. In this relationship, both compliant people are pushed or bullied by others, and neither has the necessary assertiveness to stand up for his or her rights.

A compliant person may be attracted to an extremely assertive person out of respect for that person's ability to lead and deal with conflict. While he may later feel controlled by the extremely assertive person, the compliant person may still like the relationship if the extremely assertive person is thoughtful of his needs. Both assertive and extremely assertive people may be attracted to more compliant people because they can clearly be the leader in the relationship.

Assertive people usually get along well with people who are nonassertive. However, if an assertive person is in a management or executive position and must manage a compliant person who is also in a management or executive position, the assertive boss may expect the subordinate to lead others who are a part of his area of responsibility. In this situation, the compliant manager or executive will be viewed by the assertive boss as being weak or ineffective.

Assertive people tend to get along well with other assertive people. They are best managed by leaders who are also assertive. Assertive people can comfortably lead compliant people and other assertive people. They will find managing the extremely assertive person to be quite a challenge. Assertive people are also hard for compliant people to manage.

Assertive people may enjoy being lead by an extremely assertive person if their leader is able and considerate of them, and if the leader lets them lead others in some way. Otherwise, there is likely to be a power struggle.

Extremely assertive people tend to bang heads with other extremely assertive people, especially when leadership roles have not been clearly defined and agreed upon. Two extremely assertive people usually lock horns like two big bucks in a hostile battle for dominance.

Making the Compliant Person Comfortable

To best relate to compliant people, to make them comfortable, and to reduce conflict, let them:
- Do their own work.
- Have acceptance.
- Cooperate with and submit to others.

Let them avoid:

- Arguments.
- Openly disagreeing with others.
- Criticizing others.
- Forcing others to comply.
- Stating unpopular opinions.
- Offending others.
- Dominating.
- Demanding.
- Convincing.
- Directing.
- Saying no.
- Maintaining control of others.
- Conflict.
- Being unpopular.
- Aggressive selling.
- Being pushed by others.
- Disciplining others.
- Being around arguing or fighting.
- Communicate respect for their personal work and for their cooperation.
- Let others make assertions for them or help them to make assertions.
- Put them around other compliant people where they are protected by an assertive yet benevolent person.

Making the Assertive Person Comfortable

To best relate to assertive people, to make them comfortable, and to reduce conflict, let them:

- Assert their opinions.

- Lead others.
- Have power and authority.
- Have some freedom from compliance.
- Show respect for their opinions and leadership.
- Let others handle situations where constant compliance or submission is required.

Extremely assertive people want:
- To get just what they want when they want it.
- To be able to order others to comply.
- To be in total control.
- A top leadership position.
- Absence of control from others.
- A show of much respect for their opinions and leadership.

Modifying the Compliant Tendency

A friend or counselor could:
1) Listen to the person's opinion about what he or she thinks is negative or wrong about being assertive to others.
2) Restate what the compliant person said so that person will know the helper understands.
3) Be respectful of his or her opinion.
4) As much as he or she is willing, get that person to consider what is right or good about being assertive.

Self-help for the Compliant Person

- Keep an "assertive" log. Every day write down several situations where you need to be more assertive. Consider the disadvantages of complying. Consider the benefits of being assertive. Visualize yourself successfully being assertive and the positive consequences.

- Confront fears about what would happen if you were more assertive. See how you will be safe, important, and will find happiness. See how you will successfully assert yourself. Make a specific action plan that can be accomplished.

- Try to overcome any underlying fears that may prevent comfort in differing with others. Try to overcome fears of rejection, criticism, and physical aggression. This may involve building self-esteem (chapter 5) or learning physical self-defense skills.

- Learn how to tell others what they should do and what is good or right about doing it. Learn how to tell others what they shouldn't do and what is negative or wrong about doing it.

- Tell others what you want, need, require, and expect. Tell others what is not allowed or what won't be tolerated. Say and do what needs to be said and done, even if unpopular. Say "no" more often. Dare to be different. Apply discipline more. Apply consequences to the behavior of others.

Modifying the Assertive Tendency

A friend or counselor could:

1) Listen to their opinion about their need to assert or their dislike for submission to others.
2) Restate what they have said so they will know the helper understands.
3) Be respectful of their opinion.

4) As much as they are willing, get them to consider the problems with being too assertive and the value of cooperation.

Self-help for the Assertive Person

- Keep a "compliance" log. Every day write down several situations where you need to follow the direction of others. Consider the disadvantages of being uncooperative. Consider the benefits of being more compliant and cooperative. Visualize yourself successfully following others and the positive consequences.
- Actively listen. Ask questions. Show interest. Learn about and show respect for how others think or feel. Let others fully express their ideas and opinions. Allow others more freedom to choose for themselves. Show value for others ideas, opinions, wants, and needs.
- Don't always demand in order to be in control. Let others say no when they have the right. Don't pester people who don't want or need to be pushed. Demand less often and less forcefully.
- Ask nicely. Ask before demanding and before disciplining. "Would you bring that over here, please?" "I would really appreciate it if you would do this for me." "I know you must be busy, but I need this done by 5 P.M. Could you get started now?"
- Openly disagree less. Use more tact and diplomacy. Consider the other side of the issue. Focus on the solution, not the problem. Strive for win-win solutions.
- Cooperate more. Follow the instructions of others who are in authority. Learn when to lead and when to follow.

Managing the Compliant Person

Emphasize, model, require, and reward assertive behavior. Get compliant people to share their opinions when you know they have knowledge that will help. Consider discipline for lack of assertive behavior.

Managing the Assertive Person

Emphasize, model, require, and reward compliance and cooperation. Let them know you understand their position. Explain your situation and ask them to help you work toward a win-win solution. If they are uncooperative, you may need to inform them of the consequences and enforce them.

■ Get Your Pencil—Checkup Time

To Make This Information Useful to You, You Must Apply It!

1) Write down the type of person you fit best (compliant or assertive).
2) Write down how being this way has helped and any specific problems it has caused.
3) If you have had problems with this area of emotional intelligence, then write down which solutions you will use to improve. Perhaps receive a desired reward for completing steps of your plan and for total completion.
4) Carry out the solutions you choose. Trying to change and repetition will make the action part of your character.

To Improve Relationships or to Help Others

1) Write down the type of person that someone you know fits best.
2) Write down how being this way has helped and any specific problems it has caused.
3) If that person has had problems with this area of emotional intelligence, then write down which solutions you will use to reduce conflict with that person or to build his or her performance. Perhaps he or she can receive a desired reward for completing steps of the plan and for total completion.
4) If you feel that the person is able and willing to receive this feedback, share your new insight with that person and tell him or her about what you think needs to be done.

Chapter 12

Measuring Tolerance

Tolerance is the degree to which a person is patient or willing to put up with inconvenience from others. A tolerant person doesn't anger easily.

■ Low Tolerance—the Intolerant Person

Ivan is a prosecuting attorney. He regularly becomes angry at the injustice his clients have suffered. This gives him a special motivation to correct the injustice—to right the wrong. He tries to see that his clients get the benefits they deserve and that the offending party is punished for any misdeeds. Because Ivan is also strongly assertive, he is able to verbally fight for the rights of his clients.

Strengths

Intolerant people don't accept abuse or neglect from others. They're very aware when someone has treated them harshly, unfairly, or with a lack of respect. When offended, they say they feel a flame inside that motivates them to stop the offense. When angered, they become more alert, adrenaline flows, and their muscles prepare for movement. Their anger can help them to take action.

If intolerant people are also considerate, they can become angered by injustice that is brought against others. A judge gets angry at parents who abuse their children. A store manager gets angry at an employee who has stolen from the company.

If intolerant people are verbally assertive, they can verbally fight for a cause. A mother of a child who uses drugs may be angered at drug dealers and speak out for drug control in the school. She might become an active member of Mothers Against Drunk Driving (MADD).

If intolerant people are also courageous, their anger can lead to physical retaliation. A soldier may be angered by a threat to his country and be more motivated to fight to protect it. A basketball player may be angered by a slam dunk made by the other team and retaliate by doing the same thing on the other side of the court. Salespeople can become angered at the success of their competition and work harder to win.

Different people get angry at different things. What makes one intolerant person angry may not make another intolerant person angry. Intolerant people get angry when they perceive that their needs are threatened. But different people have different needs.

A person with a self-esteem problem (chapter 5) may get angry over criticism from others. A person who is compelled to work (chapter 6) may become angry when someone makes him or her late to work. A person who is compelled to do things perfectly (chapter 7) may become angry when someone messes up her office or causes her to make a mistake. Someone who needs change in his possessions (chapter 8) will get angry if someone makes him keep the same old things. A person who needs to keep things the same (chapter 8) will get angry when someone makes him change or changes something in his environment.

Some intolerance appears to be very adaptive in most environments. Feeling anger when one is hurt is normal and healthy.

Potential Difficulties

When people are very intolerant, or if their intolerance is greater than it should be in a given environment, there's a problem. Very intolerant people get angry too easily. They become angry when others block their goals, show disrespect, or physically threaten them. The offense may be small, but they respond as if it was large. They may perceive offenses where none actually occurred. They are easily annoyed, short-tempered, touchy, and lacking in patience with even small inconveniences brought on by others.

Once angered, very intolerant people can be rebellious, refusing to cooperate with others. They can be vindictive and try to get even. They tend to hold grudges. They remember what others have done to them and think about those situations with anger. They may not let others forget what they did to offend them. They seldom forgive others for their actions.

When angered, the extremely intolerant person may become extremely critical, often saying things they don't normally feel. The highly intolerant person usually causes trouble in personal relationships whether at home, with friends, or at work.

Other character traits affect how the very intolerant person expresses anger:

1) If a very intolerant person is also low in consideration for others, he or she may neglect or abuse others when he or she is angry.

2) If a very intolerant person is also high in assertiveness, he or she will tend to verbally, and often inappropriately, fight when angered.

3) If a very intolerant person is high in courage and low in consideration for others, he or she may have a tendency to get into physical fights. Such a person also may be overly punitive in reaction to offenses he or she has received.

4) If the person is very intolerant and very low in assertiveness, that person may not communicate his or her irritation to those who are more threatening. Instead that person may take his or her anger out on others who are less likely to strike back. This is the kick-the-dog syndrome.

Ingrid was seriously criticized and neglected by her father while growing up. She was never good enough to please him and developed low self-esteem. Her father eventually left her and her mother.

During high school, a good-looking, very popular boy took an interest in her. He asked her out, and they started dating. She had a very hard time believing that someone this nice could care about her. They were married shortly after high school.

After the wedding, Ingrid became very sensitive about whether she was attractive enough. She began to worry about whether her husband might be interested in other women at his job. She also worried about whether she was keeping house well enough.

If her husband didn't go to great lengths to praise each meal, she would feel insecure and become very angry. If he picked up his clothes from their living room, she would interpret this as an affront to her cleaning skills. She would then attempt to force him to tell her what she knew he must be thinking.

When they went out to dinner with another couple, Ingrid watched her husband's every move. Once they got back home and were alone, she would interrogate him to see if he liked the other woman better than her. If her husband came home just five minutes late from work, she would already be convinced that he was leaving her for another woman. When he walked in the door, she would curse him, demand a divorce, and throw his things out the front door.

Ingrid gets so angry that she doesn't fully know what she is saying and can't stop herself. Later, she doesn't remember most of what she said and is usually sorry she said as much as she did. In the heat of anger, she accuses, criticizes, screams, and throws things.

Causes of Low Tolerance

Some people inherit a tendency to get angry easily. You can definitely trace the passing on of anger from parent to child even when the child was not raised by a natural parent.

Some intolerance is caused by chronic medical or health problems. Sudden outbursts are sometimes associated with brain injury. A person who has poor general health is more likely to be easily upset. Fatigue caused by lack of rest or sleep can cause intolerance. People who live with pain are usually less tolerant. Many women become easily angered before their period each month if they have premenstrual syndrome (PMS). Boys going through adolescence often become easily angered as a result of raging hormones.

Anger is aroused when our progress toward some desired goal is blocked, and we identify who or what blocked that goal. When we perceive an injury to our health, self-esteem, happiness, or fulfillment, we get angry at the person or thing we believe is responsible for our injury. Anger is caused when we perceive that an injustice has been committed. It usually involves blaming someone or something.

Anger usually follows this equation: Perceiving an injury, plus identifying who or what caused the injury, plus blaming the person or object, equal anger.

Intolerance may develop in an environment where anger or hostility was allowed, emphasized, modeled, required, and rewarded. Being tolerant, understanding, or patient may have been discouraged or even punished.

A generally negative attitude may cause a person to see problems as being worse than they are, which either causes the intolerance or makes it worse.

Strong intolerance may come from past hurt, abuse, or neglect. A person who was physically or emotionally abused as a child will usually have intense anger. This anger is toward the abuser but also may be directed toward others who have some qualities similar to the abuser. For example, people abused by their mothers may grow up having anger toward women in general. Those abused by their fathers may have problems with men or with authority figures.

■ High Tolerance—the Tolerant Person

Tina is a waitress at a high-quality, high-priced restaurant. The restaurant's motto is "satisfaction guaranteed." The manager tells the waiters and waitresses "the customer is always right." Sometimes the cooks delay a customer's order and the customer becomes angry. Tina is patient with the customer's irritation and shows that she understands the customer's situation. She also does not get mad at the cooks. When a customer complains about the food, Tina is apologetic and doesn't talk back in a defensive manner. She will take the food back to the kitchen twice, if necessary, to please the customer. If the situation gets out of hand, the kitchen manager or the restaurant manager intervenes. They are less tolerant than Tina.

Strengths

Tolerant people, as the name indicates, tend to be tolerant of inconvenience from others. They are not easily offended and are slow to anger. They usually don't become angry when others block their goals, show disrespect, or offer physical threat.

Tolerant people demonstrate patience when others inconvenience them. They're unlikely to get into heated arguments or fights. When inconvenienced, they usually don't try to get back at the person who bothered them.

Tolerant people don't usually blame others or hold grudges. They seem to find a way to be understanding toward the person who has bothered them. They try to forget what others have done to them and don't think about those situations with anger. They don't continue to complain about what others have done to them in the past. They tend to forgive, cooperate, and try to get along well with others.

Potential Difficulties

Very tolerant people may tolerate inappropriate behavior, including abuse or neglect. They may put up with unfair treatment and let others block their goals, show disrespect, or even threaten them. They may not take action to stop or prevent inappropriate behavior. A very tolerant manager may tolerate inadequate performance from an employee.

The very tolerant person tends to deny and hold in anger, causing significant stress. People who deny anger find it unacceptable to admit that they are angry. When they are inconvenienced, they may act as if nothing bothered them. As they hold in their anger, internal stress builds up.

Tolerant people may have been very hurt by others and yet smile and act as if nothing wrong was done. They may be too ready to make excuses for others. If someone drops a brick on their toe, they might smile and say, "That's okay, it was just an accident."

They don't express irritation to others when their needs are abused, largely because they aren't aware of feeling irritated. Repressed anger may build up over a period of time, and the person who commits the last inconvenience may get all of the stored up anger dumped upon him or her.

Repressed anger may be tightly controlled and almost never expressed, usually resulting in physical symptoms like stomach ulcers, tension headaches, sleep disturbances, or skin disorders. Repressed anger can also cause depression.

Teresa's father was an alcoholic who when drunk would beat her mother. Teresa was hurt a few times trying to protect her mother but soon gave up. If her father didn't like what Teresa said to him, he would cuss at her and slap her. When Teresa was eight years old, her father left her and her mother. Despite the repeated beatings and other forms of abuse, the mother begged him not to leave.

Teresa, without conscious intent, married a man who was very much like her father. Though she thought he was only a party drinker while they dated, Teresa soon realized after they were married that her husband was an alcoholic. He regularly stayed out at bars and came home drunk. Then he would hit her, push her, and throw her into things. He took extended trips he said were business trips—some as long as two weeks—and wouldn't say where he was. He called home every now and then and always demanded to know exactly where she had been. She was expected to stay at home all day and wait for him to return. She had to ask permission to go shopping or to see a friend. During their twenty years of marriage, he never kept the kids, never mowed the yard, and never helped at home. To control her, he kept the car keys, credit cards, and money.

Teresa quietly put up with this behavior for twenty years. Only twice during this period of time did she threaten divorce. When she came for counseling, she wouldn't admit to feeling anger toward her husband. However, after several sessions, she began to get in touch with a flood of angry feelings toward her father, her mother, her husband, and toward herself. Before counseling, she never had a safe place to express these feelings and so had kept them a secret even to herself.

Causes of High Tolerance

Children are born with different levels of tolerance. Some children don't express irritation or anger even when the expression of anger would be accepted in the home. You can see genetics at work more obviously in animals. Pit bulls are usually born with a temper. Take their bone and you might lose a finger. Golden retrievers generally are very tolerant. Children often ride them, hit them, or take their food without retaliation by the dog.

High tolerance may have developed in an environment where being tolerant or patient was emphasized, modeled, required, and rewarded. Being angry or expressing anger may have been discouraged or punished. In some families, the parents don't express irritation. Nor do they allow their children to say what bothers them.

A generally positive attitude (chapter 4) may cause a person to see problems more positively, which would lessen the tendency for anger. An excessively positive attitude may result in denial of anger.

A person may not express anger because of fear of criticism, fear of rejection, or fear of physical violence. These fears may come from direct experience or may have been learned from others.

■ Identifying Tolerance

The following is a typical conversation that reveals a person's level of tolerance.

Question: "Tell me about something someone did that really bothered or upset you."

Answer: "Someone scratched my new Corvette."

Question: "Who did this and how did it happen?"

Answer: "The paperboy scraped it with his bicycle."

Question: "How did you feel about what happened and about the person?"

Answer: "I was furious with him! That Corvette was hard for me to buy!"

Question: "After you noticed [the scratch on the car], what did you say or do?"

Answer: "I got in my car, chased him down, and screamed at him for five minutes!"

Question: "How do you feel about the situation and the person now?"

Answer: "I'm still furious! I'll have to have the whole quarter panel repainted!"

Very intolerant people will tend to display a short temper, strong angry feelings, and either anger-motivated behavior or strong internal pressure. They may still be angry about a past event. Tolerant people will most likely have some anger, but it is likely to be appropriate to the offense. The behavior will also be reasonable for the offense. Very tolerant people will show no signs of anger even when something very hurtful has happened to them. In the same situation, highly tolerant people would respond: "Cars are going to get scratched sometimes anyway."

If a person is intolerant, as he talks about things that made him angry, you may notice a scowl on his face. His lips may purse tightly. Blood rushing to his face may make his nose and cheeks red. Some people squint and clinch their jaw. Other bodily muscles may show tightness. They may clench their fists or bang something. Their tone of voice may get harsh, tense, and loud. The tolerant and highly tolerant people will show fewer of these signs.

Other people, including references, may be able to tell you how the person handled things that bothered him and whether there were any signs of anger or intolerance.

■ Solutions to Problems

Tolerance and Jobs

Some intolerance is needed in careers such as competitive sports and in being a courtroom attorney, a soldier, or a policeman. In management, some intolerance of poor performance is often helpful. Presidents brought in to companies for the purpose of a turnaround are significantly intolerant. It is seldom helpful, however, to have very low tolerance.

Tolerance is a characteristic that is helpful in relating pleasantly to the public. It's a good characteristic to have in jobs such as customer service, salesclerk, bank teller, receptionist, pharmacist, barber, nurse, or physician. However, very high tolerance only seems to work in certain settings where the person is not dealing with others or is expected to tolerate just about anything that happens.

Tolerance and Relationships

Very tolerant people tend to be most comfortable with tolerant people. In this relationship neither is inflicting anger on the other. Yet, the tolerant person has enough ability to be irritated by abuse and is willing to do something about it.

Very tolerant people need people who will not allow abuse to occur. In a marriage where someone should protect the daily needs of the couple, very tolerant people actually seem to be least compatible with other very tolerant people. In this relationship, both very tolerant people are abused or neglected by others.

Very tolerant people are not comfortable with intolerant people. They don't like the anger and conflict that the intolerant person tends to produce. When very tolerant and intolerant people get together, the very tolerant person probably didn't make the match or know about the incompatibility.

In a rare circumstance, a very tolerant person who also has low self-esteem may be attracted to a very intolerant person because she feels she deserves the anger that is directed toward her. This person is usually a female who had an abusive father and who perhaps subconsciously chose someone just like her dad.

Both intolerant and extremely intolerant people may be attracted to more tolerant people because they can express their irritation and anger without receiving much retaliation. However, if an intolerant person is in a management or executive position and supervises a person who is also in a management or executive position, the intolerant boss may dislike how the tolerant person allows others to perform poorly in their areas of responsibility.

Tolerant people tend to get along well with both tolerant and very tolerant people. They may not enjoy relating to very intolerant people but can as needed. Extremely intolerant people tend to get into angry fights with each other. Like two porcupines, whenever they get close, they hurt the other person. Many couples who come in to counseling because they incessantly fight do so because they are both intolerant.

Making the Intolerant Person Comfortable

To best relate to very intolerant people, to make them comfortable, and to reduce conflict:
- Identify the particular things that upset them.
- Don't do the things that trigger their anger.
- When they are angry, give them space and time to cool off.
- Don't press them when they are angry.
- Do your best not to offend or inconvenience them.
- Let others handle situations that involve being patient with inconvenience.

Making the Tolerant Person Comfortable

To best relate to very tolerant people, to make them comfortable, and to reduce conflict:
- Do not make them express irritation or anger toward others.
- Do not let others take advantage of them.
- Get other people who will express irritation to others, who will not tolerate inappropriate behavior, and who will step in to correct it.
- Let them avoid being around angry, conflict-oriented people.
- Communicate respect for their personal work and for their cooperation.
- Put them around other tolerant or very tolerant people.

Modifying the Intolerant Tendency

A friend or counselor could:

1) Listen to their opinion about their need to express anger.
2) Restate what they have said so they will know the helper understands.
3) Be respectful of their opinion.
4) As much as they are willing, get them to consider their problems with excessive anger and the value of patience.

Self-help for the Intolerant Person

- Keep a "tolerance" log. Every day write down several situations where you need to be more patient with others. Consider the disadvantages of getting very angry. Consider the benefits of being more tolerant. Visualize yourself successfully demonstrating patience and the positive consequences.
- Work through past hurtful situations that triggered the anger. The first part of this involves identifying the anger-producing events and expressing anger about those events.
- When angered, answer three important questions: Does this prevent me from being healthy or safe? Does this prevent me from being highly respectable? Does this prevent me from being happy in life? The answer to all three is usually no.
- Understand how the situation and people were reasonable given the circumstances. Look at the situation more positively. Forgive the situation, thing, or person that

triggered the anger. Do this sequence for each significant anger-producing situation.

- When angered, take several slow, deep breaths. Flex and release tense muscles. The breaths and muscle stretching are relaxing and also provide a brief pause, which is necessary to allow the anger to significantly decrease. Counting to ten also might help.

- Strive to speak slowly and in a low tone of voice. This not only is courteous to others but is also calming. Speaking fast and in a loud, harsh tone can actually generate more anger all by itself.

- Work out a solution to avoid or to correct situations that tend to trigger anger. It's harder to get rid of anger if abuse or neglect continues to occur.

- Avoid spending time thinking about the offense, how bad it was, and about how you would like to get back at others.

- If the anger is a result of a low self-esteem, then work to build the self-esteem.

- Correct any medical or health-related causes for anger such as not getting enough sleep.

Modifying the Tolerant Tendency

A friend or counselor could:

1) Listen to their opinion about what they think is good or right about tolerating inappropriate behavior from others.

2) Restate what the tolerant person said so she will know the helper understands.

3) Be respectful of her opinion.

4) As much as she is willing, get her to consider what is right

or good about admitting and communicating irritation to others and about preventing abuse or neglect.

Self-help for the Tolerant Person

- Keep an "intolerance" log. Every day write down several situations where you need to be more intolerant. Consider the disadvantages of tolerating these situations. Consider the benefits of letting others know what you dislike and stopping it. Visualize yourself successfully expressing your irritation and the positive consequences.
- Confront fears about what would happen if you expressed more irritation or tried to stop abuse. See how you will be safe, important, and can find happiness. See how you will successfully express yourself. Make a specific action plan that can be accomplished.
- If you are a very tolerant person in a relationship with a physically dangerous person, expressing irritation to this particular person should be questioned.
- Tell others what is not allowed or what won't be tolerated.
- If you have been denying and suppressing anger, learn to admit feeling anger. Learn that anger is normal and acceptable. Learn to express anger in appropriate ways to others. Mention the situation that bothered you and your feelings about it.
- Once you become more aware of your anger, you may need to work through past hurtful situations that triggered the anger. The first part of this involves identifying the anger-producing events and expressing your anger about those events.
- As you begin to get in touch with your denied anger,

you may experience a sudden rush of angry emotions and actually need to learn how to manage anger. If this happens, refer to the section on modifying the intolerant tendency.

- If you don't express anger because of fear of criticism, rejection, or physical violence, you may need to work on self-esteem (chapter 5), broaden your social acquaintances, or take a self-defense course.

Managing the Intolerant Person

Emphasize, model, require, and reward understanding, patience, and forgiveness. Consider punishment for excessive expressions of anger.

Managing the Tolerant Person

Emphasize, model, require, and reward expressing irritation and preventing inappropriate behavior. Consider discipline for tolerating poor behavior.

■ Get Your Pencil—Checkup Time

To Make This Information Useful to You, You Must Apply It!

1) Write down the type of person you fit best (intolerant or tolerant).
2) Write down how being this way has helped and any specific problems it has caused.
3) If you have had problems with this area of emotional intelligence, then write down which solutions you will use to improve. Perhaps receive a desired reward for completing steps of your plan and for total completion.
4) Carry out the solutions you choose. Trying to change and repetition will make the action part of your character.

To Improve Relationships or to Help Others

1) Write down the type of person that someone you know fits best.
2) Write down how being this way has helped and any specific problems it has caused.
3) If that person has had problems with this area of emotional intelligence, then write down which solutions you will use to reduce conflict with him or her or to build that person's performance. Perhaps he or she can receive a desired reward for completing steps of the plan and for total completion.
4) If you feel that the person is able and willing to receive this feedback, share your new insight with that person and tell him or her about what you think needs to be done.

Chapter 13

Measuring Consideration for Others

Consideration for others is how understanding, thoughtful, helpful, honest, and responsible the person is.

■ Low Consideration—the Self-willed Person

Seth is the owner and operator of a profitable computer store. He makes sure that the hardware and software products purchased for his company are of sufficient quantity, cost him as little as possible, and are available when he needs them. Seth tries to get the most product for the lowest possible price. He may get suppliers to compete with each other to drive down the price he pays. Or he may talk with an individual supplier and negotiate for a lower price. Seth resells the computer products at a substantially marked-up price—as high as his customers will pay without going somewhere else to buy. Seth's motto is "buy low, sell high."

Clearance items are sold as is, with no explanation of any defects that are known to exist. Seth tells his salespeople to get the customer to buy the most expensive product possible, even if the customer could happily use a much less expensive version. "After all," Seth tells his sales staff, "the customer really needs the better product. They just don't know it."

Strengths

Self-willed people are strongly motivated to take care of their own needs. They feel strongly about what they want and strongly dislike others blocking their goals. They are not content to let others inconvenience them or take advantage of them. In a competition, they want to come out on top. If they give something, they expect something in return. They only do those things that will have a direct benefit to them.

Self-willed people want to be in control of situations so that they can get what they want. They won't let the opinions of others get in the way of their goals. Self-willed people expect others to do what they want them to do. If they are also assertive, they may be very direct in letting others know what they expect. If they are not assertive, they may find more indirect ways of getting what they want. Self-willed people don't worry much about the feelings or experience of others. They're more free from feelings of guilt than others who are more considerate.

Potential Difficulties

Extremely self-willed people have little concern for others. They may neglect or abuse others to meet their own needs. They usually strive for "I-win-you-lose" outcomes and have little empathy for others. They tend to have a poor understanding of others' feelings and needs and are generally insensitive to the feelings of others.

If you want to tell your problems to someone, don't pick an extremely self-willed person. They are not concerned about others' problems and needs. They find it difficult to serve the needs of others without significant reward in return. "Loyalty" is given only to those who can meet their needs.

Very self-willed people tend to be unhelpful, selfish, dishonest, and irresponsible. They can be too opportunistic and take advantage of others. In fact, our research shows that those who have been convicted of theft are almost always very self-willed.

Lack of consideration can be linked to war between countries and to virtually every crime ever committed. It's a prime factor as the cause of divorce and of child abuse. Lack of consideration keeps the courts and prisons full. In fact, without consideration for others, the world would be one big war zone where those with more power would take from those who have less power.

Perhaps 50 percent or more of the things that others do which annoy you are a result of a lack of consideration—the driver who cuts in front of you, the neighbor who plays music too loud, the employee who sues the company based on false accusations.

Stan was single and twenty-two years old. He graduated from a technical school, majoring in electronics. Being a physically attractive person and verbally articulate, he interviewed very well. Based on these qualities, he was hired to run a small, one-person repair center for electronic equipment such as fax machines and photocopiers.

Shortly after he was hired, a serious situation developed in the repair department. Customer after customer began to complain that their machines had been kept too long for repair. Many machines didn't work right even after being serviced.

Stan generally promised that a machine would be fixed within a week and returned to the customer. When an inventory was taken, it was discovered that some equipment had been in for repair for as long as five months. Some customer equipment had been "cannibalized" for spare parts. That is, parts were stolen from one customer's machine and sold as new parts to another customer. Some machines that had been at the shop the longest had virtually been gutted.

Stan was guilty of property theft as well as stealing time from his employer by not working when he said he was. For months, Stan had led everyone in his company to believe that he was taking care of business. In reality, he had been doing very little and was simply drawing a paycheck. He knew this scam wouldn't last, but he stayed with it as long as his employer allowed. Stan's business practices had definitely crossed over the line from taking care of his needs to seriously abusing the needs of others.

In our previous chapter, we told the story of Teresa. Her husband, Sonny, was so selfish, that he deserves his own story in this chapter.

When Sonny courted Teresa, he consciously did a selling job. He did everything he could to make her fall in love with him. He spent a lot of money on her, bought her gifts, and concentrated his time on her. He praised her almost constantly. He found out what she liked and acted interested in those things. He had only dated her for a few weeks when he asked her to marry him. She was unsure about marrying so soon, but she gave in to his constant pressure.

While Sonny had been a party drinker while they dated, it became obvious after they were married that he was a full-fledged alcoholic. He stayed out at bars most of the night meeting new people and would very frequently come home drunk. On these nights he would hit Teresa, push her, and throw her into things.

During his extended "business trips," he frequently slept with other women. He called home every now and then and always demanded to know exactly where Teresa had been. He boasted to friends that his wife was "all his" and "just for him."

Sonny demanded that Teresa stay at home all day and wait for him to return. When he did return, he spent his time bragging about his big business success. He didn't want to listen to her talk about the air conditioner that needed repair or about one of the children who was sick.

Teresa had to ask permission to go shopping or to see a friend. Most of the family's extra money was spent on Sonny. He had a fancy car, expensive clothes, a gold watch, and traveled and dined out frequently. During their twenty years of marriage, Sonny never kept the kids, never mowed the yard and never helped at home. To control Teresa, Sonny took her car keys, her credit cards, her money, etc. This relationship was the epitome of an "I-win-you-lose" relationship.

Causes of Low Consideration

Low consideration for others and selfishness is how most infants behave at birth. They demand that others meet their needs. They are not yet capable of knowing how others feel in response to their actions. They don't naturally offer to give or to help. Children have to learn to be considerate.

Low consideration can be further developed in an environment where selfishness was allowed, emphasized, modeled, required, and rewarded. Being considerate or giving may have been discouraged or punished. Low consideration also may stem from a harsh environment where taking care of oneself is necessary to ensure the meeting of physical or emotional needs.

■ High Consideration—the Considerate Person

Clint is a police officer. Since he was a little boy, he dreamed about being a policeman. He wanted to catch "bad guys" and help people. Clint went through the police academy where he learned a lot about the law, police procedures, driving a patrol car, self-defense, and firing weapons. Once he was assigned his beat, he became a very good policeman. He helped keep the streets safe by giving tickets to those who drove dangerously. He apprehended the robber of a convenience store, protected a woman from being mugged, recovered a stolen car, and put drug dealers in jail. He never used his job as a way to abuse others and didn't give in to occasional attempts to pay him off.

Some people use this job as a way to exercise their hostility or simply as a way to earn a living. In all his time as a policeman, however, Clint saw himself as a public servant. His primary desire was to help others. Sometimes helping someone meant fighting someone else, even hurting that person, if necessary. He disliked hurting offenders, even when it was necessary. Clint's focus was on delivering justice and helping those who needed it.

Note that to do this job, Clint also had to be courageous (chapter 9) and assertive (chapter 11).

Strengths

Considerate people are thoughtful of the feelings and needs of other people. Considerate people care about others and are willing to listen to people talk about their problems. Possessing empathy, they are sensitive to how others feel and are understanding of the difficulties that others experience.

They tend to do things that are helpful and are determined to do what they have promised to do. They tend to be generous with and giving of their time, money, or other resources.

Considerate people are honest, responsible, and loyal. People who are moderate to high in consideration try to balance meeting their own needs with meeting the needs of others. They strive for win-win solutions to problems. They are fair, just, and tend not to show unfair partiality to others.

Potential Difficulties

Highly considerate people may do too much for others and neglect their own wants and needs. They may actually get into win-lose situations where others win and they lose. They tend to give away the store. In a situation where they should sell at the highest possible price or buy at the lowest possible price, they may not drive for the best advantage. Instead, they want to make an equitable deal, resulting in lower sales or higher cost. Ironically, without intending, very considerate people may neglect the needs of a company or family to do what they feel is the right thing to do for an individual.

Very considerate people may care to the point that they feel deep hurt for others who experience physical or emotional pain. They may be so sensitive as to actually feel others' feelings. They may feel very guilty when they put their needs before others or when they do what they consider to be wrong.

Colleen is a missionary. Although she's licensed as a nurse-practitioner and could be pulling in a significant income, for the past ten years she's worked in a small health clinic in a remote third-world country. She's thousands of miles from her family and friends. Colleen receives only enough pay to live on and receives supplies once a month brought in by a small plane. She sleeps in a room with no air-conditioning or electricity. Most of her day is spent tending to the medical needs of the village. In her spare time, she teaches Bible studies at the center of the village. Over the past ten years, Colleen has saved thousands of lives and has improved the quality of life for many others. Her reward is knowing that she is helpful and is doing what she views as the right thing.

Chris is a very uncommon businessman. His business—employee and personal counseling—is totally oriented around helping others. Much of the personal counseling he does for free. Many of the employees he hired to work at his company were hired with full knowledge that they needed help and might not perform well for a while.

Every Sunday night and on some Wednesdays, he taught Bible studies at both the county and state prisons. While other people were out at the lake, playing golf, or working in their yards, Chris prepared his lesson, made popcorn, bought cokes, then taught his lesson to prisoners. He developed a personal relationship with most of the men in his group. No one paid him for these efforts.

When prisoners he knew were released, Chris often let them live at his house, gave them money, helped them get a job, and bought them clothes. He would try to get friends and business acquaintances to give the men jobs. If no one he knew had a position available, he helped the men to decide where they could apply for a job. He also paid them to paint his house, fix his cars, cut the grass, or do carpentry work. He often paid more than a job was worth.

Many of the inmates learned a better way of life from Chris, and as far as we know did not return to prison. Some used Chris's kindness as an opportunity to steal from him. One inmate only halfway got the right idea. Out of appreciation for what Chris had done for him, he offered to show Chris's son the proper way to hot-wire a car.

Chris also gave his time to an older sister who was disabled and couldn't get out of her house. For many years, he would visit her, talk to her about her problems, bring her food, and take her to the doctor. She was difficult to get along with, but he went anyway, not because she made him, but voluntarily.

Chris and his wife had saved up for many years to buy a small houseboat. They took it on a couple of trips and really enjoyed it. However, Chris found out about a children's home that was in need of recreation, so he gave the boat to the home for children, personally towing it for two thousand miles to deliver it.

Chris took several families into his house. At one time there were three families (totaling eleven people) living in his small house, all using one bath.

Chris's life was one sacrifice after another. Once when he and a business partner split up, he gave up all of his stock in the company. When buying a house, he paid what the person was asking for it without making a lower offer. He wanted to make sure that the older couple selling the house would get what they needed out of the sale.

It's hard to include Colleen and Chris in a section called "Potential Difficulties" because of the tremendous good that people like them do for others. The "difficulties" involve hardships that they personally suffer in doing what they believe is good or right. I don't believe that any of the native children whom Colleen treated would say she did the wrong thing in leaving her friends and money to save their lives.

Sometimes people who spend so much time helping others don't take what they need for themselves. Although Chris's family respected what he did for others, they really wished that he had saved more time and more money for them. Chris didn't save a lot of money or keep a very good insurance policy. When he finally became very ill, he only received minimal care.

Causes of High Consideration

High consideration develops in an environment where being considerate or giving was emphasized, modeled, required, and rewarded. Being selfish may have been discouraged or at least not encouraged. Those who are considerate have usually been treated with consideration while also being taught to be considerate of others.

Sometimes people who have been abused or neglected decide that no one should have to suffer like they have. They commit themselves to helping others, especially in the way they would have wanted to be helped. A person who was emotionally abused as a child may decide to become a family counselor. A person who grows up being bullied may learn self-defense skills and later teach them to others.

■ Identifying Consideration

Ask the following questions: "Tell me about a time when you wanted something to be one way, and someone else wanted it to be another way." "What happened?"

Listen to hear whether the person did it totally her way (possibly self-willed), shared or compromised (possibly considerate), or let the other person totally have his or her way (possibly highly considerate).

If she did it all her way, what was her reason for believing she should be the one to have what she wanted? If she shared, compromised, or totally gave in, what was her reason? Was it because she wanted to give (considerate), because she didn't want to but was intimidated by the other person (low assertiveness), or because she realized that what the other person wanted was really the most reasonable way?

Then ask, "As quickly as possible, list five ways that you give to or help others."

And ask, "As quickly as possible, list five ways that you try to get or receive something from others."

There is no simple way to visually examine a person you are talking with and tell how considerate that person is. You might be able to see a genuine smile from a considerate person. Considerate people may raise their eyebrows and have good eye contact, showing their interest in you (however, considerate people who are not sociable may not pass this test).

Considerate people may listen to your needs or problems, showing a caring interest or a concern.

If you're really desperate to "see" consideration in an interview, you might watch how a person responds to contrived situations such as your spilling your water or dropping a pencil at his feet. Notice whether he does not help, grudgingly helps, or cheerfully helps.

To truly judge consideration, you must be able to see how the person responds to actual situations: selfishly or in a sharing, caring or sacrificing way. You can see how that person answers certain projective questions, or ask other people, including references, about that person. Or you can use the Simmons Personal Survey, which will be discussed later in the book.

■ Solutions to Problems

Consideration for Others and Jobs
....

Being self-willed is particularly helpful in situations where others may mistreat the person if that person doesn't look out for himself, such as being a prison guard. It is also needed in job situations where the company expects the person to meet its needs, even at the expense of others, such as in high-pressure sales.

Most executives and salespeople are self-willed. Executives must get workers to do the most work for the least amount of pay. Buyers are usually expected to drive the purchase price down and to get the most from the vendor. Salespeople are usually expected to present the positives of their product or service, minimize the negatives, and get the best price possible.

Note that we are not saying that to be in business you have to be selfish. However, most successful business people are rather self-willed. Beating the competition usually means finding a way to get more money from the public than others who provide a similar product or service. Making a big profit usually means charging customers more than you really need to charge them.

Judges should be considerate. So should nurses, doctors, pastors, rabbis, counselors, teachers, clerks, and virtually anyone who is in a service-oriented job.

While a high degree of consideration is a requirement for some types of work, consideration is also a necessary requirement for appropriate social relationships in general. Every employee should have enough consideration to be trustworthy to his or her employer.

Consideration for Others and Relationships

Very considerate people tend to be most comfortable with other very considerate people. These people will share beliefs about giving and helping others. In this relationship, neither is selfishly taking from the other.

Very considerate people may not realize it, but they may need a somewhat less considerate person to make sure that they don't give too much and sacrifice their needs or the needs of their family.

Very considerate people are not comfortable with self-willed people. They don't like the selfishness and lack of giving that self-willed people tend to practice. Very considerate people probably would not choose to have a relationship with a very self-willed person unless they were trying to help them.

Self-willed people want to be around other self-willed people in some settings and around considerate people in other settings. For instance, self-willed people may want the people they rely on to manage or sell to be self-willed people. Self-willed executives will want the managers below them to expect a lot out of their employees. Self-willed sales managers will want their salespeople to drive for the best sales price. Self-willed people are comfortable with other self-willed people, if these other people clearly do not try to take advantage of them.

Self-willed people also enjoy relationships with considerate people who allow them to meet their needs most of the time. A self-willed boss will enjoy having a considerate secretary who tries to meet his or her every need. A self-willed husband will enjoy a considerate wife.

Two self-willed people in a relationship that has not been clearly structured may find that they argue over who will get what they want, especially if there are limited resources. Imagine two thirsty self-willed people finding only one canteen?

Making the Self-willed Person Comfortable

To best relate to very self-willed people, to make them comfortable, and to reduce conflict:

- Give them what they want.
- Let them do what they want to do, the way they want to do it, when they want to do it.
- Make them aware of what they will personally get from doing what you want or how they will be personally inconvenienced by not doing what you want.
- Give them respect for the profitable deals they make.

- Let others handle situations where someone must listen, give, be sensitive to feelings and needs, offer help, and genuinely care for others.

Making the Considerate Person Comfortable

To best relate to very considerate people, to make them comfortable, and to reduce conflict, let them:

- Help others.
- Give to others.
- Know how they have helped.
- Act in an honest manner.
- Be loyal and responsible.
- Give them appreciation for their thoughtfulness and for how they have helped.
- Don't take from them what they need to live, be safe, or happy, or they will be less able to meet your needs.
- Let others handle situations that involve being opportunistic, hurting others feelings, or being less than honest.
- Put them around other considerate or very considerate people.

Modifying the Self-willed Tendency

A friend or counselor could:

1) Listen to their opinion about their need to have what they want.
2) Restate what they have said so they will know the helper understands.
3) Be respectful of their opinion.

4) As much as they are willing, get them to consider the problems with selfishness and the value of consideration for others.

Self-help for the Self-willed Person

- Keep a "considerate" log. Every day write down several situations where you need to be more considerate of others. Consider the disadvantages of being selfish and the benefits of being more considerate. Visualize yourself successfully demonstrating caring or helpfulness and the positive consequences.

- When feeling the need to take, answer three important questions: Does being without this prevent me from being healthy or safe? Will it prevent me from being highly respectable? Will it prevent me from being happy in life? The answers to all three are usually "no." Look at the situation more positively. Find another way to get what you need that does not abuse or neglect someone.

- Listen, learn, and respect how others feel. Respect others' needs and rights. Try to understand how others feel or would feel if you get what you want. Strive to treat others as you would want to be treated.

- Learn the joy of giving. Help and give more. Show loyalty and responsibility. Be honest and truthful. Avoid "I-win-you-lose" relationships. Strive for "I-win-you-win" relationships.

Modifying the Considerate Tendency

A friend or counselor could:

1) Listen to their opinion about what they think is good about helping, giving, or sacrificing.

2) Restate what they say so they will know the helper understands.

3) Be respectful of their opinion.

4) As much as they are willing, get them to consider what is right or good about taking care of themselves. Consider what could be negative or wrong about not taking care of themselves, giving too much, etc.

Self-help for the Considerate Person

- Keep a "self-help" log. Every day write down several situations where you need to be more self-willed and less giving. Consider the disadvantages of giving too much. Consider the benefits of taking care of yourself and your right to do so. Visualize yourself successfully looking out for your interests and the positive consequences.

- Confront attitudes like: "Others' needs are more important than mine," "I'm only good if I am giving something," "I used to be so bad. I need to give everything now to make up for my past," and "I can only feel good about myself when people show appreciation for what I have done."

- Evaluate what would happen if you took care of your interests better. See how you will be safe, important, and can find happiness. See how you will successfully express yourself. Make a specific action plan that can be accomplished.

- When helping others, strive for a balance in meeting all needs involved and avoid the possibility of focusing on some needs while forgetting others.

- Value your own wants and needs more. Get and do more for yourself. Let others do more for themselves. Learn that doing for others isn't always helpful to them.

"I-lose-you-win" relationships actually teach others to be selfish. Strive for win-win relationships.

- If you don't take care of your needs due to fear of criticism, rejection, or physical violence, then you may need to work on your self-esteem, broaden your social acquaintances, or take a self-defense course.

Managing the Self-willed Person

Emphasize, model, require, and reward consideration, fairness, and honesty. Consider punishing excessive expressions of self-interest. Be wary of their motives. Make sure that they do not have the opportunity to harm you. Be ready to refuse a request or a demand from them.

Managing the Considerate Person

Emphasize, model, require, and reward getting more from others and doing more for self. Discourage being too giving or sacrificial.

■ Get Your Pencil—Checkup Time

To Make This Information Useful to You, You Must Apply It!

1) Write down the type of person you fit best (self-willed or considerate).
2) Write down how being this way has helped and any specific problems it has caused.
3) If you have had problems with this area of emotional intelligence, then write down which solutions you will use to improve. Perhaps receive a desired reward for completing steps of your plan and for total completion.
4) Carry out the solutions you choose. Trying to change and repetition will make the action part of your character.

To Improve Relationships or to Help Others

1) Write down the type of person that someone you know fits best.
2) Write down how being this way has helped and any specific problems it has caused.
3) If that person has had problems with this area of emotional intelligence, then write down which solutions you will use to reduce conflict with him or her or to build that person's performance. Perhaps he or she can receive a desired reward for completing steps of the plan and for total completion.
4) If you feel that the person is able and willing to receive this feedback, share your new insight with that person and tell him or her about what you think needs to be done.

Chapter 14

Measuring Sociability

Sociability is the tendency to meet people, spend time talking, and be group oriented.

■ Low Sociability—the Reserved Person

Ruth was an Internal Revenue Service agent. Her responsibility was to check the calculations that people made on their tax forms for truth and accuracy. She worked in a cubicle that separated her from other workers and was only able to chat with coworkers on her breaks and at lunch. Otherwise, Ruth was expected to stay at her desk and read through the tax forms. Many people would find this work lonely, but Ruth liked the solitude. When she did take a break or have lunch, she usually chose to spend the time alone.

Ruth was married and had two children who were grown and living on their own. She saw them every few months when they would visit, and she talked to them on the phone a couple of times a month. Ruth's husband was a salesman who was gone much of the time, but again, she didn't mind. At home, she stayed busy knitting, reading books, cooking, cleaning, and watching television.

Strengths
....

The reserved person doesn't feel the need for much company or conversation. Reserved people don't waste time with endless and nonproductive chatting. You won't find them socializing with a group in the kitchen when there's work to be done.

Reserved people are comfortable doing work either alone or with one or two people. They usually do their work quietly, drawing little attention to themselves. Reserved people are more comfortable working with things, data, or ideas than with people. They enjoy the lack of social interaction involved in jobs like bookkeeper, records clerk, lab technician, or artist.

Reserved people often pursue individual tasks or goals. If they are athletic, they may pursue sports such as singles tennis, track, swimming, long-distance running, weight lifting, or walking alone.

If reserved people are also assertive, they'll be involved in verbally influencing others. There are many reserved yet assertive people in management positions. However, their conversation will only involve what is necessary to solve a problem or to accomplish a specific goal. They may be verbal when meeting a need but still quite reserved and emotionally distant.

Often, reserved people are introspective. They are primarily concerned with their own thoughts and feelings. They think about their situations, their work, and their plans. They are usually refreshed by having time to themselves.

Reserved people like boundaries that can separate them from others. The boundary may distance them from others or may involve walls or partitions. They also tend to want privacy regarding their feelings, their problems, and their personal lives.

Potential Difficulties

Reserved people are not usually outgoing and sociable. They generally don't seek others' company and conversation. They tend to have few acquaintances, although they may have a few close friends. They are loners. Very reserved people need a lot of privacy. They may isolate themselves from others.

Reserved people don't feel comfortable interacting with a large group of people. They can feel drained or tired by long periods of mixing with others. In purely social settings, they may be at a loss for what to say. Even when they are around others, they may feel isolated. They can feel most lonely in a crowd where others are enjoying conversation and they are not.

While reserved people may find it easier to not build acquaintances on a regular basis, their lack of social contact also may make them feel lonelier than they want to feel. Yet the immediate discomfort involved in developing new relationships may cause them to continue their isolation.

Because the reserved person does not seek out conversations, other people may feel that they are not liked, valued, cared for, or appreciated. Others may perceive reserved people as being cold or distant.

Actually, the reserved person may care very deeply for others but has difficulty expressing it. If the reserved person is also considerate, his or her caring may be expressed in more tangible ways, such as giving financial assistance, fixing a broken object, or being loyal and dependable.

Very reserved people may appear colorless and uninteresting. They tend to have difficulty being entertaining or showing enthusiasm to others. They are generally not expressive of their emotions.

Randall lived in a small beach house in a quiet community. His house was well off the road, and to reach it you had to drive down a long, wooded drive. The beach house was also a distance from the water and was surrounded by a thick growth of trees. The large lot was totally secluded—out of sight from other houses in the area.

Randall didn't hold a job and lived on his disability pay. He was single, didn't date, and had no friends. Although he was very religious, he didn't attend church. He was uncomfortable in crowds and around people he didn't know. He spent his time watching television, listening to the radio, and walking on the beach—mostly at night when no one was still out. He also would do his grocery shopping at night when the store was almost empty.

When he was growing up, Randall's parents had constantly argued and often brought him into the middle of their arguments. His parents were highly assertive and intolerant. He had been teased for his shyness by children at school. A girl he had loved called off marriage with him just before the wedding date. He had a long list of job failures as well. Randall had much pain in his past and was permanently withdrawing from all social contact.

Causes of Low Sociability

Children are born with differences in sociability. It is commonly believed that most girls tend to learn social and conversational skills earlier and better than most boys. This of course is not to say that every girl is more socially adept than every boy.

Even among all girls or among all boys, you see social differences in infancy. Some boys are quiet and not as responsive to their parents. Other boys babble, particularly in response to their parents.

Low sociability develops in environments where being quiet or reserved was emphasized, modeled, required, or rewarded. Being outgoing or sociable may have been discouraged or punished.

Being quiet and reserved also may have developed as a result of hurtful social encounters involving rejection, criticism, neglect, or abuse. The person may have withdrawn from others to prevent possible future abuse.

■ High Sociability—the Social Person

Sonia is a flight attendant who works as part of a crew. Sonia meets and greets each person who boards the airplane. She is usually smiling when conversing with the passengers and helping them store their carry-on baggage. During the flight, she provides them with dinner, snacks, drinks, or magazines. Sonia demonstrates safety procedures that would be necessary in an emergency. She shows a genuine interest in brief, light conversations. At times, she may need to reassure passengers of their safety. Sonia also enjoys social meetings, excursions, and parties when she's at a layover destination.

Strengths
....

Social people are interested in and responsive to other people. They like to be with and around others, whether at work or at play. They affiliate and want to be part of a group and also like to spend time with their friends.

Social people like to meet new people. They're comfortable showing an interest in others and in introducing themselves. They tend to be good at "small talk" and starting conversations. The social person is stimulated and energized by talking with or associating with other people. Social people make many contacts and acquaintances.

It is easy for social people to express their thoughts and feelings. They're usually articulate and make a good impression. They spontaneously show emotions and tend to be gregarious and entertaining.

Social people enjoy social interaction, social recognition, being popular, friendship, conversation, proximity to people, personal and informal relationships, group membership, group activities, and identity with the group. They usually have a lower interest in working with objects or with data.

Potential Difficulties
....

In most settings, being sociable does not create a problem. However, social people do not fit well in environments where they're isolated from others or expected to be quiet for long periods of time. They may feel depressed when they are alone. Working in a private office with a closed door with little personal contact is not suitable for the social person. In such an environment, they would either be unhappy or might talk more than their manager would want.

Very sociable people need attention from others. They want popularity, public recognition, and group-activity. Conversation may take priority over getting a job done or over responsibilities. Most people feel that the very sociable person talks too much. These are the party animals. They need to have the stimulation of being with people, talking, and joking. They may go from one party to another.

Shawn was a manufacturer's sales representative. He worked eight- to ten-hour days as a traveling salesperson, constantly calling on customers. In between interviews, he was on his cellular phone with other customers. While he was articulate and liked by most customers, many felt he wasted their time with idle conversation.

Shawn was a party animal. Even after all of the social contact that his job involved, he still wanted more. At night, he would find out where things were happening and be there. It might be a bar, a dance hall, or a gambling casino. When at these places, he would constantly meet new people. He constantly stayed out late and barely got enough sleep.

His wife was very displeased with Shawn's behavior. Besides being concerned about his fidelity, she found that she got to spend very little time with him. Her idea of a nice evening was to have dinner at home, watch a movie on television, or go shopping. Being with one person all the time was very difficult for Shawn. He felt confined by his wife's way of relating. Even when Shawn took his wife out with him, he often wound up meeting other people and lost focus on her. These incompatibilities finally bothered both of them enough that they strongly considered a divorce.

Causes of High Sociability

As we discussed earlier in this chapter, children are born with some differences in sociability. Social tendencies also develop in environments where being talkative was emphasized, modeled, required, and rewarded. Being quiet or reserved may have been discouraged or punished.

Excessive talking may be motivated by an excessive need for attention or recognition. The attention or recognition may reassure the person that they are worthwhile. This problem stems from poor self-esteem (see chapter 5).

Social excitement is almost addicting to some people. They get a high out of meeting new people and talking about new things. People who need to be with new people all the time tend to also have an excessive desire for change (see chapter 8).

Identifying Sociability

Ask the person to describe a day or perhaps a week of his behavior. Don't tell that person what you are looking for. Just keep him talking about what he does.

Reserved people will have few personal conversations and will engage in fewer recreational activities with others. Social people will have friendly conversations and enjoy activities with others. Excessively social people may be constantly mixing with others.

Observe how these people handle conversations with you. Are they impersonal or withdrawn? Are they friendly? Do they talk your ear off about some meaningless subject?

Ask other people, including references, about whether the person is reserved, outgoing, or excessively talkative.

■ Solutions to Problems

Sociability and Jobs

Reserved people are comfortable doing work either alone or with one or two people. They are more comfortable working with things, data, or ideas than with people. They enjoy the lack of social interaction often found in jobs like a bookkeeper, records clerk, lab technician, or graphic artist.

Social people enjoy the kind of interaction found in jobs like salesperson, politician, teacher, host or hostess, receptionist, bank teller, actor, and news reporter.

Sociability and Relationships

Reserved people normally feel more comfortable around and have fewer conflicts with other reserved people. They do not tend to expect more talk or affiliation than other reserved people are comfortable giving. However, a reserved person may benefit greatly by having a sociable person take responsibility for meeting, greeting, and rapport building.

Social people normally feel more comfortable around and have fewer conflicts with other social people. However, a social person can benefit from a reserved person who is expected to stay low-profile and do research, calculations, or other behind-the-scenes work for him or her.

A reserved person may be very attracted to a social person because the social person is exciting and is able to initiate the relationship with him or her. A social person may initially like relating to a reserved person because the social person can do as much talking as he or she wishes and can control the direction of conversations. However, there is a tendency over time for reserved and social people to develop conflicts.

Reserved people eventually may be viewed as boring or as party poopers by social people. They may be threatened by social settings such as parties or family reunions that social people enjoy.

Social people may be viewed as not willing to focus on reserved people, giving too much of their attention to others. They may feel stifled or confined by the lack of social contact that reserved people want to maintain.

These incompatibilities can be successfully handled in any of three ways:

1) The reserved person can become more social.

2) The social person can become more reserved.

3) The two people can learn to appreciate the value of one being reserved and the other social. They can also respect and appreciate one another's unique qualities.

Making the Reserved Person Comfortable

To best relate to very reserved people, to make them comfortable, and to reduce conflict:

- Get to the point quickly when in a conversation with them.

- Keep the conversation task-oriented.
- Don't pry about their personal life or about their deep feelings.
- Allow them time to be alone.
- Respect their need for physical boundaries.
- Let them choose solitary activities such as jogging or sewing.
- Include them, and don't reject them, but don't force them to socialize.
- Take the initiative to start a conversation with them but talk only as long as they seem interested.
- If they must go to a social gathering, stay with them and help them to interact.
- Don't make them stay at these settings for a long time, since mingling and small talk are tiresome to them.
- Give them respect for not wasting time in useless conversation.
- Let others handle situations that involve building rapport, meeting and greeting others, conversation, or entertaining.
- Let others know that the reserved person does care, even if that person does not always show it.

Making the Social Person Comfortable

To best relate to social people, to make them comfortable, and to reduce conflict:

- Spend some time talking with them.
- Listen to what they have to say.
- Try to be a friend.

- Let them have plenty of social interaction, including talking to others and activities with others.
- Let them be part of a group.
- Let them be with or work around others.
- Give them attention.
- Give them respect for their ability to relate to others.
- Let others handle situations that involve being quiet or isolated from others.
- Put them around other social people.

Modifying the Reserved Tendency

A friend or counselor could:

1) Listen to their feelings about not personally interacting with others.
2) Restate what they have said so they will know the helper understands.
3) Be respectful of their opinion.
4) As much as they are willing, get them to consider the problems with isolation and the value of affiliation and intimacy.

Self-help for the Reserved Person

- Learn to understand and to respect the value of the social person.
- Keep a "social" log. Every day write down several situations where you need to be more social with others. Consider the disadvantages of being reserved. Consider the benefits of being more social. Visualize

yourself successfully socializing and the positive consequences.

- When feeling the need to avoid social situations, answer
  three important questions: Does socializing prevent me
  from being healthy or safe? Will it prevent me from being
  highly respectable? Will it prevent me from being happy
  in life? The answer to all three questions is usually no.
  Look at the situation more positively.
- Try to overcome any underlying fears that may prevent
  comfort in conversing or affiliating with others.
  Overcome fears of rejection, criticism, and physical
  aggression. This may involve building self-esteem
  (chapter 5) or learning physical self-defense skills.
- Recognize your need for people.
- Be more outgoing and sociable. Learn to show interest
  in others, introduce yourself, conduct small talk, ask
  questions, and listen. Share feelings and opinions, and
  initiate joint activity.

Modifying the Social Tendency

A friend or counselor could:

1) Listen to their opinion about what they think is good
   about talking and affiliating.
2) Restate what they have said so they will know the helper
   understands.
3) Be respectful of their opinion.
4) As much as they are willing, get them to consider what is
   right or good about being quiet or reserved.

Self-help for the Social Person

- Consider what could be negative or wrong about talking or relating too much.
- Keep a "reserved" log. Every day write down several situations where you need to be more reserved, more private, or more quiet. Consider the disadvantages of talking too much. Consider the benefits of being more reserved or private. Visualize yourself successfully being reserved and the positive consequences.
- Evaluate what would happen if you were more reserved. See how you will be safe, important, and can find happiness.
- Develop social outlets outside the job in order to be able to tolerate isolation that may be part of a job. If you are in a relationship with a reserved person, find some additional appropriate social outlets.
- If you also have a low work ethic, be careful to stay on task and don't chat when work needs to be done.
- Confront attitudes like: "I'm only good if people notice me or include me." If you are excessively talkative, you may need to work on your self-image so you won't need constant affirmation from others.
- Understand and respect the quieter tendencies of the reserved person.

Managing the Reserved Person

Create an environment where conversing or affiliating is emphasized, modeled, required, and rewarded. Being reserved or withdrawn may be discouraged or punished.

Managing the Social Person
....

Emphasize, model, require, and reward being quieter or affiliating less. Being too talkative or spending too much time
relating to others may be discouraged or punished.

■ Get Your Pencil—Checkup Time

To Make This Information Useful to You, You Must Apply It!

1) Write down the type of person you fit best (reserved or social).
2) Write down how being this way has helped and any specific problems it has caused.
3) If you have had problems with this area of emotional intelligence, then write down which solutions you will use to improve. Perhaps receive a desired reward for completing steps of your plan and for total completion.
4) Carry out the solutions you choose. Trying to change and repetition will make the action part of your character.

To Improve Relationships or to Help Others

1) Write down the type of person that someone you know fits best.
2) Write down how being this way has helped and any specific problems it has caused.
3) If that person has had problems with this area of emotional intelligence, then write down which solutions you will use to reduce conflict with him or her or to build that person's performance. Perhaps they can receive a desired reward for completing steps of the plan and for total completion.
4) If you feel that the person is able and willing to receive this feedback, share your new insight with that person and tell him or her about what you think needs to be done.

Section Two

Uses of the Survey

At this point, you have learned much about emotional intelligence in general and about the thirteen specific facets of emotional intelligence. You have had an opportunity to do a basic evaluation of yourself and others. You have also been able to set some goals for personal development, improvement of relationships, and for helping others.

As exciting and valuable as this has been, there is *much more* insight and help available by personally processing the Simmons Personal Survey. The Survey's evaluation will be much more objective and precise, going beyond the blind spots that most of us have about ourselves and about those we relate to.

For each character area, the Survey shows the *exact* level of your feelings and behavior, makes a comparison to eighteen standard job norms, shows how your character affects job performance, shows the full range of your feelings and behavior, shows how you present yourself to others, reveals the direction you are now moving, and provides suggestions for improvement.

The Personal Survey gives you much more insight and help in your personal development, improvement in relationships, ability to help others, and career guidance—finding the place where you fit best. The versions of the Survey that are available to individuals are the EQ Profile and EQ Insights.

If you want to get a Survey on yourself or on someone you know, use one of two methods:

1) If you have access to a computer that can get onto the Internet, go to www.EQhelp.com. Simply follow the instructions for completing the Survey on our web site.

2) Send the card located at the end of this book with the current fee to: Simmons Management Systems, P.O. Box 770265, Memphis, TN, 38177-0265. We will then mail you an answer blank. After filling it out, mail or fax it to us, and we will mail or fax your results back to you.

■ Business and Organizational Uses of the Survey

In the last two chapters of this book, we will discuss how the Survey can be used in organizations to improve productivity and to reduce costs. If you are a business owner, a CEO, are in human resources, do business consulting, counsel people, or manage people, these chapters will be of particular interest to you.

In chapter 15, we discuss successful employee hiring and promotion. We discuss how to hire new employees and how to select employees from within the organization for promotion.

In chapter 16, we discuss developing successful employees. We cover personal character development, particularly in an organizational setting.

Finally, in the Appendix, we give some information about the Simmons Personal Survey and list some of our authorized

Associates. If you are interested in using the Survey in organizations for hiring, employee development, etc., you need to contact one of these Associates.

Successful Employee Hiring and Promotion

The success of every organization depends upon the quality of the people within the organization.

People make the financial and operational decisions in an organization, and they make the products. People sell the products, and they deliver the service. People have been responsible for the degree of success a company has today, and people will determine the success of a company in the future.

While people cause success, they also are capable of causing failure. Poor employees cause high turnover, wasted selection time, absenteeism, labor disputes, wasted supervisory time, lowered productivity, waste and costly delays, theft and shrinkage, employee-related lawsuits, poor customer service, loss of customers, and decreased sales and profits!

Consider, for example, the staggering costs of employee turnover. The U.S. Chamber of Commerce reports that it costs from ten to twenty times an employee's weekly wage to turn an employee over. The costs are even higher for skilled employees, managers, executives, etc.[1] The weekly wage for a semiskilled employee who makes $6 an hour would be $240. Ten times this weekly amount is $2,400. Twenty times this weekly amount is $4,800.

Effective employees are only obtained in two ways:

1) Effective employees must be hired or placed where they fit in the organization.

2) Effective employees are developed (i.e. trained, managed, counseled) to fit their jobs.

While this point may seem obvious, consider its implications. An organization's success depends upon the ability to hire and to develop good people.

$$\begin{array}{l} \text{Hiring the best people} \\ \underline{+ \text{ developing these people}} \\ = \text{organizational success} \end{array}$$

While the success of an organization depends upon hiring and developing the best employees, this often does not happen.

■ Hiring Problems

According to a national study done by the U.S. Department of Labor, 50 percent of applicants who are hired stay only six months in their job. While some of those who leave their jobs were promoted, the vast majority of those who left their jobs quit or were fired. Another Department of Labor study revealed that more than 60 percent of all workers stay at an organization less than five years.[2] These studies show that the hiring success of most companies is no better than flipping a coin! Why does this happen?

Hiring Problem #1

Inaccurate interview information. A study by Reilly and Chao (1982) reported a correlation of .19 between predictions of job performance based on interviews and actual job performance.[3] John Hunter and Ronda Hunter (1984) show this correlation to be only .14.[4] That is, predictions of job performance based on interviews are very inaccurate.

Many people can interview better than they can perform. Many applicants read books or receive training on how to perform in an interview so that they *look* very attractive. They learn how to dress, how to answer the interviewer's questions, and how not to answer them. Many people have become much better at interviewing than they are at doing their jobs.

Some people, however, do not look as good in an interview as they actually perform. This happens when their social skills are not well developed. They may be hardworking and technically proficient, but they are not sociable, verbally articulate, or assertive enough to comfortably express their opinions. Yet, put these people in the laboratory, at their computer, or onto their forklift, and they perform very well.

Hiring Problem #2

Inaccurate information from the resumé/application. Poor employees are often hired because their resumés or applications tend to be overstated. Many people have companies write their resumé for them. Applicants may have read one of hundreds of books on resumé writing. The resumé very often makes even small accomplishments look like major achievements. In many cases, the information is simply false. Unfortunately, people can overinflate their descriptions of past performance because they know that their previous employer won't dispute their claims.

While most people overinflate their resumé, there are a few who do just the opposite. Some people are very modest. They don't feel comfortable "tooting their own horn" about what they have done, and they amazingly will actually minimize reports on their successes. Others who are very low in self-esteem will even put themselves down. Still another type of person is not able to express himself well on paper.

Hiring Problem #3

Inaccurate information from references. The study mentioned above by John Hunter and Ronda Hunter also shows that the correlation between predictions of job performance based on reference checks and actual job performance is only .26. Predictions of job performance based on reference checks are very inaccurate.

Many job references will only give you dates of employment and tell you the position the person held. Others will try to be very positive about the person. Very few will tell you about the problems they had with their past employee.

Most employers who withhold information do so because they are afraid of being sued by the employee either for defamation or for invasion of privacy. There are many lawsuits every year where employees sue their past employer for harming their chances to get another job.

Some references, especially friends, withhold negative information because they don't want the applicant to be angry with them. A few references withhold negative information because they, shortsightedly, are trying to help the applicant. They don't realize that they may only be helping the person to get a job that may end up in failure. They also may not be thinking about the consequences to the prospective employer.

While most references are either uninformative or too positive, there are a few who are too negative. Some previous bosses are hostile, negative, unfair, or critical. Some are also daring enough to tell you what they think about the applicant. These references are not objective or impartial. They can really mislead you. And, heaven help the applicant who has had more than one of these bosses who must be used as a job reference.

While we are on references, it should be noted that some of them cannot even be found. The reference may have worked with the applicant many years ago but has also left the organization, with no forwarding address.

Problems with getting accurate information from the interview, from the resumé, and from references make it very difficult to see the applicant the way he or she really is. Many of the applicants who look good, simply aren't. On the other hand, some of the applicants who look bad, are really good.

How often have you seen this happen? You are trying to hire a good employee to fill a specific job. The person's application or resumé looks good. They interview well. Their references are either quiet or positive about them. They are hired. Weeks or months later, you find that this employee is performing far worse than was expected. What kinds of performance problems did this create? How expensive was this situation to the company?

What is needed is an accurate, thorough, dependable, and

easy way to measure character. This is what the Simmons Personal Survey was designed to do.

Like an X ray, the Survey easily and accurately measures the most important job-related character tendencies: Energy, Stress, Optimism, Self-esteem, Commitment to Work, Attention to Detail, Need for Change, Courage, Self-direction, Assertiveness, Tolerance, Consideration for Others, and Sociability.

The Simmons Personal Survey will reveal just what each applicant is like, penetrating the facade they may attempt to present. In just a few minutes time, you can know more about a person's character than you would by observing them for several years! You can actually get to know people better than they know themselves!

For each character area, the Survey shows how the person tends to feel and behave, makes a comparison to a standard or customized job norm, and shows how that person's character affects job performance, her range of feelings and behavior, how she tries to present herself, and the direction she is now moving in. Suggestions for improvement are offered.

With the Survey, you can assess strengths and weaknesses relative to any job and predict the level of job performance. Consistently hire the best people for any job: executives, managers, salespersons, workers.

The Personal Survey, with its ability to measure emotional intelligence, provides a solution to hiring and development problems and, therefore, significantly contributes to the success of any organization.

Note: Promotion is "selection" from within the ranks. While

you may feel you know much about an employee because of the way he has responded to one job, his adequacy for another job can be quite different. For instance, many of the qualities that make an excellent worker (compliance, desire for structured work, etc.) make for a very poor manager. The Survey will show you readiness for promotion. You can see how well your employee fits a variety of work norms—both present and projected.

■ Character Measurement Produced Tremendous Turnover Reduction

by Pat Sumpter
Management Consultant

I began using the Personal Survey in 1990 as store manager for a supermarket chain. At first, I was the strongest "naysayer" of all. I thought tests were hogwash, just a waste of time and money.

Before we began using the Simmons Personal Survey, our turnover rate was a crippling 172 percent, and the cost of hiring and training an entry-level worker in the supermarket industry was one thousand dollars each. Management costs rose exponentially from that.

We started out by doing Simmons Personal Surveys on all existing management. When Wes Crane [another Simmons Associate] went over the results of my own Survey, I was amazed. "How could you possibly know that from a test?" I asked. I could see the value of knowing that much about an applicant before we hired him, and I was sold on it!

We totally integrated the Simmons Personal Survey into our Human Resource procedures, using it specifically at three levels.

1. **Hiring:** After job applicants were narrowed down to three, all were given the Survey. We used it for every position, from entry-level throughout management.

   Since we originally began by giving the Survey to all of our existing management, we could see how the Survey scores related to success in our stores. We knew what we were looking for in an applicant, and we could choose the one who would fit best.

2. **Promotion:** We used the Survey to help us know which employees were really ready for promotion.

   The Survey showed us whether they had good emotional energy, commitment to work, and attention to detail. Then we looked to see if their tolerance and consideration for others was balanced with the appropriate decisiveness and assertiveness to be a manager.

   We promoted the best candidate, but the benefits of using the Survey went far beyond that. All candidates had the opportunity to discuss their Survey with us. Often those who had not been promoted would say, "I really want to move up into management. What is it that's holding me back?" We would go over their Survey, showing them specific areas that they could work on.

   Providing this assistance in their development proved to be extremely cost effective. Before long we were promoting entirely from within.

3. **Department Manager Annual Review:** Each year the department managers took the Simmons Survey and

compared it to their results from the previous year. In a meeting with the store manager, they would review and acknowledge the improvements they had made. The employees had the opportunity to make suggestions about what they thought needed improvement, then the store manager made his suggestions. Together they developed specific goals for the next year.

4. **Results:** Within eighteen months, the Survey was the key to reducing turnover—from a crippling 172 percent to a manageable 70 percent. This development process has double benefits of reducing turnover and increasing effectiveness.

■ A Ten-Step Hiring Process Using the Personal Survey

To predict job performance you must know two important things. You must know the job requirements, *and* you must know the person's characteristics that are relevant to the job.

1) First, *carefully* study the job to be filled.

a. Know the job, title, and rank in the organization (e.g., secretary to the general manager).

b. Consider all tasks and results to be achieved. For example, for the job of general office secretary, the person could be responsible for word processing, answering the phone, screening and sorting mail, maintaining customer files, etc.

c. For each task, determine exactly what must be done and how you want the person to do the task. Word processing may involve using a Dictaphone, using Windows 95 and Word for Windows 6.0, doing some basic editing, saving and storing files in an organized manner, and printing out the results. Both speed and accuracy are very important.

d. For each task, determine what the job requirements would be. The secretary would ideally need one year of experience with a Dictaphone, knowledge of and one year of experience in using Windows 95 and Word for Windows 6.0, a mastery of English and of writing skills, typing speed of eighty words a minute — error-adjusted, etc.

e. Determine how you will measure the person's ability to do the tasks involved in the job. For the secretary, you may use a word processing test that actually gets her to make use of the Dictaphone. You may use a test to measure her knowledge of Windows and of Word for Windows. Or, you may wish to rely on looking at her grades on Word 6.0, etc. from her business-skills school.

f. For each task, consider the type of character required: the level of stress they can have, the need for a positive or a negative attitude, how much work is required, how much attention to detail, change vs. routine, physical comfort and safety vs. discomfort and risk, decision making vs. following structure, leading vs. following, conflict vs. cooperation, consideration vs. self interest, sociability vs. being alone or quiet.

For example, to do the word-processing part of the job, you will probably want the secretary to have: a high commitment to work; high attention to detail; the ability to handle routine work, sitting in one place; an interest in a comfortable, protected setting; a desire to normally follow directions, but be able to use her judgment at times (as in editing); and the ability to be quiet while keying in data, etc.

Determine which capabilities are required as well as which capabilities are denied. If a person's character is not "strong enough" to do part of the job, to some degree there will be anxiety and failure. If the person is "stronger" than what the job calls for, that person may feel confined and need to do more than the job allows.

g. In addition to measuring the job, also consider the character and competency of the immediate supervisor. The right supervisor can help many people to succeed when they would otherwise fail. The wrong supervisor can substantially lower the performance level of both good and poor employees.

Domineering, insecure supervisors can seldom tolerate much independence or initiative from those under them. Conversely, they may get reasonable performance from those who are poorly able to direct themselves. This also means, however, that they tend to limit the contribution of the more capable workers to those things they direct the subordinate to do. Further, they may easily drive away their best workers.

On the other hand, supervisors who are too permissive, who allow their people to do much as they please and exercise very little supervision or direction, need competent, self-directed workers if anything is to get done.

The best way to get this type of information is to compare a recent Personal Survey of the supervisor to those considered to work under him or her.

h. Based upon your evaluation of the job and of the supervisor, you can then select one of our standard job norms. If you process the Simmons Character Inventory, you will know to look at the score for this norm at the bottom of the graph.

i. Another way to determine exactly which characteristics are related to success in a given job is to develop your own validated job norms. Basically this involves identifying individuals who do a specific job very well, those who do the job poorly, and those who do it moderately well. Survey each of these people, and you will be able to see a success pattern and a failure pattern in the scores. With assistance from one of our Associates, this pattern can be converted into a job norm that can be used each time you use the Survey.

j. Write out all of the job requirements and also write up a hiring procedure for each person hiring for this position. The hiring procedure will communicate what to look for in the resumé/application, what to ask references about, what to do in the employment interview, etc.

2) Announce the job opening. This can obviously involve newspaper ads, internal job postings, etc. It is a good idea to let potential applicants know what some of your most important requirements are so that you will not be bothered by too many people who are not qualified looking for the job.

3) Have the applicant give a resumé with references and/or fill out an application. Ask for working relationships with

former supervisors, peers, or subordinates. Personal reference checks should *not* be close friends, pastors, or lawyers unless no other sources are available. Neighbors of long-standing are better references. Also, ask your candidate for adverse references. Plan on calling people they worked for and who worked for them. Also, call people you may know in that company. Be sure to get a written release to contact their current employer. If important for the job, educational transcripts and records of previous testing (e.g., a typing test) could also be asked for at this time.

4) Some resumés and applications will show information that will let you know that you do not want to hire the person. The person may have too little experience, too little education, want too much money, etc. If the resumé/application is negative enough to let you see that the applicant clearly would not succeed, then inform the person of your decision. (See the "nonacceptance" message below.)

If the resumé/applications (transcripts, previous testing, etc.) are positive, contact these applicants to have them take the Personal Survey and any other testing necessary. At this point, you also may want to measure specific learned skills and knowledge relative to the position, perhaps in the form of a written or performance test.

If the person has never done the tasks they will be expected to do, find out how adequate his or her mental abilities are relative to the position. Tests like the Differential Aptitude Test are short enough to be used in the hiring process, yet are also reasonably thorough. Measuring physical fitness or judging physical appearance may be done if it is definitely job related.

As you gather any or all information on the applicant, give it a rating. For example, use a 1 to 5 rating. 1 is very poor; 2 is poor; 3 is average; 4 is above average or good; 5 is very good. The secretary's typing skills of eighty words a minute (error-corrected) might be given a 5 rating.

5) Obtain an interpretation of the Simmons Personal Survey. Based on the results, develop specific questions to ask of references. Also get ready to ask the applicant about certain job-related strengths and weaknesses that the Survey reveals.

6) Applicant interview:

   a. Setting: Use a private and comfortable room and prevent others from interrupting the interview. Ideally, have seats arranged so that you sit facing the interviewee with no desk in between the two of you.

   b. Time: Plan to take one to two hours. Less time gives the interviewee more ability to put up a facade. More than one interview with you or with someone else also increases your chances of seeing the real person.

   c. Build rapport: Greet interviewees in a friendly, interested manner. Be sure to smile and to shake their hand. Offer them water or coffee. Perhaps engage in some very brief small talk.

   d. General interviewing rules:

      1. In general, use open-ended questions that require explanation and not simply a "yes" or "no."

      2. Allow silence. Give the applicant time to struggle with an answer.

3. Control the direction of the conversation, but get them to bear the burden of sharing information. Talk around 10 to 20 percent of the time. Let them talk 80 to 90 percent of the time.

4. Get them to tell you what they did, not merely what their work group did.

5. Make them be specific and fully explain their answers. With each question, get specific details and examples.

6. If all positive information is being shared, ask for problems or difficulties.

7. Only ask questions that are job related. You can always get the applicant to explain how he or she will perform each of the duties necessary for the job.

However, *do not ask* about the applicant's: gender, disabilities or handicaps, family, marriage, child care arrangements, age, arrests, race, religion, national origin, sexual preference, citizenship, or type of military discharge.

You *can ask*: if they can legally work in this country; if they have ever been convicted of a specific legal offense that would relate to the job (e.g., stealing—if the job involves handling cash); if they would need any special accommodations to allow them to do the job.

8. Ask the same questions of each person being interviewed for a particular job.

e. Have them discuss the following areas:

Experiences before employment: What they liked to do the most. What they liked to do the least. Which tasks they did. What they learned. What they did well. What they did less well. Which tasks they liked. Which tasks they disliked. Which kinds of people they liked. Which kinds of people they disliked.

Summer and full-time work: What they did. What they learned. What they did well. What they did less well. Which tasks they liked. Which tasks they disliked. Which kinds of people they liked. Which kinds of people they disliked. Their reason for leaving each job. What have they had the most experience doing?

Education: Which subjects they did well. Which subjects they did less well. Which subjects they liked. Which subjects they disliked. Which kinds of people they liked. Which kinds of people they disliked. How much education have they had? What did they major in? What degrees do they hold, if any?

How they spend their leisure time: What they like to do the most. What they like to do the least. What tasks they do. What they have learned through leisure activities. What they do well. What they do less well. Which tasks they like. Which tasks they dislike. Which kinds of people they like to spend time with. Which kinds of people they don't like to spend time with.

Aspirations and goals: Do they have a desire to do some particular thing with their life? What would they like to be five years from now, ten years from now, twenty years from now? How much do they want to reach these goals? Are there things that would prevent them from reaching their career goals? How they feel about this job and about this organization. Explain.

What they see as being their strengths relative to the job.

What they feel are their limitations relative to the job. In chapters 2 through 14, we listed questions you can ask that can help you to verify character. Verify both positive and negative characteristics that the Survey shows.

f. Get the applicant to actually perform what they are to do. Possibly make up simulations where they perform a task, solve a problem, etc.

g. Tell the applicant what will happen next in the hiring process.

h. After the interview, you will be able to further screen out a number of potential employees.

7) Check references (job, educational, and social). As with the applicant interview, only ask job-related questions.

a. Find out how well the reference knows the applicant and what their relationship is.

b. Find out in general, how the reference feels about the applicant. Positive? Negative? Why?

c. Get the reference to tell you what the applicant's duties were. As each specific duty is discussed, find out what was done well and what was done poorest. (Get actual examples.)

d. Verify both positive and negative characteristics found in the Survey. Use your Survey results as hypotheses to check out: "Mrs. (reference), I have been informed by another source that (applicant) had trouble making decisions on his own. What can you tell me about that?"

e. Ask if this person is eligible for rehire.

f. If the reference gives you little information or all positive information, use the following methods:

1. "Let me ask you (reference) to put yourself in my place. Would you want to hire this person without some background information?"

2 "If a person gets a job he can't handle, it will mean just another black mark on his resumé. I know you don't want to contribute to that."

3. "We are honestly looking at how to best manage him. Help us get to know him so that we can help him get off to a good start."

4. "What I hear you saying is that he is *almost* perfect. Everyone has some difficulties. What does he have trouble with?"

5. "Mr./Ms. (reference), we simply are not going to hire (applicant) until we know more about him. Your apparent desire to *help* him may keep him from getting the job. I'm asking you to help (applicant) by helping us."

6. "Mr./Ms.(reference) I don't quite understand. According to what you have told me, (applicant) has no areas for improvement."

7. Use a point-blank question: "To your knowledge, has he ever come to work while drinking?"

g. In recording your information, be sure to write down just what the reference says on one side of the page, and list your conclusions and interpretations on the other. Keep all information from one person separate from those of others.

h. After the call, draw hypotheses about the reference and record your own conclusions. This will call for your determining the character of the reference while calling. Determine if they are telling half-truths, all the truth, exaggerating, defending their own biases, etc. Be sure to ask one reference to give another reference. You may have to ask the applicant for permission to contact these additional references.

i. Possibly check records like worker's compensation claims, criminal record, motor vehicle report, and credit history. There are companies that specialize in reporting on this type of information that can help you. Again, you should only check this information if it is actually job related.

8) Draw your conclusion about the adequacy of the applicant's character for the job. Combine this evaluation to what you know about his or her skills, knowledge, etc., and make your decision. Also consider how much employee you will be getting for the money he or she expects to receive. Ideally, you should meet with all of the other people in your organization who have interviewed the applicant. Compare your findings. Select the candidate with the highest rating and negotiate salary. Get a commitment.

9) Contact other applicants. Maintain a good relationship with your future job applicant pool while avoiding

unnecessary hiring disputes. Send a letter or call on the phone: "Thank you for considering employment at (your organization). We enjoyed meeting you, and your application materials were given every consideration; however, after much difficult evaluation, we have selected another candidate to fill our position. Best wishes."

10) Once the new employee is hired, communicate your findings to those who will manage that employee. This is like providing the manager with the owner's manual so that she or he can know how to best manage the new employee. For example, some manager trainee candidates may need to begin to work on their self-direction, others on their assertiveness. Some will respond better if they receive praise. Others will be bothered by much praise.

■ Character Stories

The following are true stories from some of our Associates. They show the value of understanding character through using the Survey.

The Survey Helps Hire the Right People, Reducing Turnover

by Charles T. Kenny, Ph.D.

A large metropolitan hospital reduced its critical-care nursing turnover from 65 percent to 15 percent within eighteen months using the Simmons Personal Survey!

In 1983, turnover in critical-care units was a national problem. It may *still* be a national problem, but for one large metropolitan hospital, it's not anymore. In fact, they have consistently held it down for seventeen years.

When we began working with them, turnover among critical-care nurses was running at 65 percent. We used the Simmons Personal Survey along with our *Insight* methodology to identify the factors that were causing high turnover. Two basic patterns emerged:

1) The Negative Leader. We identified a group of nurses who shared specific negative character traits. They were embittered people whose energy was turned against themselves, against their coworkers, and against their employer. These nurses were operating in a leadership capacity, either formally or informally. They might be a floor supervisor or not, but by the sheer force of their personalities, length of tenure, etc., they were operating in a leadership role.

   They would take new nurses off to the side and indoctrinate them with their own belief system about the hospital administration, management, and other nurses. Who are the good guys, who are the bad guys; who wore white caps, who wore black caps. They indoctrinated new recruits with their bitterness, and it spread like a disease through the unit.

2) The Emotional Character of a Successful Critical-care Nurse. The emotional makeup of a successful critical-care nurse is very different from nurses in other areas. The ideal CCU nurse does not need a lot of personal feedback or expressions of appreciation, etc. She's not

going to get it in the CCU from the patients, who are all wired up and unconscious, a certain percentage of whom are going to be lost.

If a person goes into nursing because she wants to serve and help other people, she gets gratification when she sees the results of her efforts; she gets some "attaboys." If she needs them, then she doesn't belong in CCU because she's not going to get them.

Results: Once we described the "Negative Leaders," it was easy to identify them. Everyone knew who they were, they just didn't realize the affect they were having on other nurses in the unit. They needed to be isolated or moved out. To her credit, the hospital vice president was able to devise a plan that accomplished this without any "major surgery." Then they began using the Survey to staff the CCU with nurses whose character fit the success profile identified by the Survey. In six months they could see a marked improvement in the unit.

Within eighteen months, the whole situation had been turned around. They reduced their critical-care nursing turnover from 65 percent to 15 percent.

Now they use the Survey to identify the emotional profile of all nurses right out of nursing school as well as new hires and in-house transfers. It allows them to place a nurse in the OR, general nursing, CCU, psychiatric, etc., by matching the appropriate character traits to the needs of the unit.

They solved their critical problem and have continued to use the Simmons Survey for hiring, placement, personal development, and promotion for seventeen years.

Using The Survey for Promotion Decisions Dramatically Reduced Turnover

by Wes Crane

We couldn't find an answer to our manager turnover problem in the deli and bakeries. We always promoted experienced, good workers, yet they became stressed-out, unsuccessful as managers.

A colleague at a seminar told me the Simmons Personal Survey was helping them choose people for jobs that required leadership. After a two-hour conversation with Jack Simmons, I was convinced that this might work for us, but I had doubts that it could do *all* of this.

We started using the Survey for choosing managers in our delicatessens. Up to that point, we had been turning over a deli manager every two months. In the six months after we started using the Personal Survey, we did not turn a single manager. After starting to use the Survey, we only had two turnovers in a three-year period of time. This was a tremendous success for us because it had been such a serious problem area before.

During that period of time, we saw the value of using the Survey in choosing the right people for promotions. From then on, we gave everybody who was up for promotion in any department the Simmons Survey.

Often, we surprised ourselves with the person we promoted. But it basically proved to us that the Survey was valid, and the predictions we would make in an interview were not always the correct ones. We had been looking at work and responsibility rather than leadership traits. The best sandwich maker got promoted to the manager and failed—not because of technical knowledge, but because of character.

Good Work Experience Doesn't Necessarily Make Good Managers

by John Beane

A manufacturing firm was preparing to open a new plant. They had gotten word of a gentlemen who was a twenty-five-year veteran of the industry, highly thought of by everyone. They had tons and tons of good reports on this guy.

When I did his Survey interpretation, there were several things that bothered me. For instance, he was neither goal oriented nor a self-starter. This led me to believe that he would probably not be a very good leader to take this plant from start-up to the high production rate they expected. And yet their main reason for hiring him was the fact that they felt he could get it up to speed really quickly. But in the absence of strong management characteristics, I said I wouldn't recommend hiring him.

The president of the company called me and said, "Well, you know, I've got such good reports on him from all of these people in the industry. You're the only one who says don't hire him." And I said, "Well, it's your money, and you can do whatever you want, but here's what's going to happen. If you hire this gentlemen, within nine or ten months you're going to let him go because he's not a self-starter. He's not going to lead the plant, and you're going to do his job for him or it won't get done."

They called two weeks later and said, "We've decided to go against you're advice and hire him because he had such a good reputation from the industry." I said, "That's fine. It's your money. No problem."

I did about four months of training sessions with the new supervisors and this plant manager, teaching them how to set goals, etc. On the side, from the supervisors, I was hearing, "Well, you tell us all this neato stuff, but the plant manager never does anything about it."

So I began to very firmly set specific objectives for the manager, with instructions to report back on his progress at the next training session. He'd come back next time and say, "Well, I didn't have time, we were just so busy." Nothing ever got done.

Before long, the only way I could find the president of the company and the vice president of manufacturing was to go down to the new facility, because that's where they were, each running a half of an assembly line and doing the job of the plant manager. After about six months like this, I said to the president, "It looks to me like you have a decision to make. Are you going to be the plant manager, or are you going to be the president of this company? Because if you're the president, I would expect to find you in the president's office, not running a line at this plant."

Three weeks later, they finally decided that the manager was not capable of doing the job, fired him, and found someone else. This time they heeded my Survey recommendations and chose a man who was successful as a manager and figured they could teach him how to build their product.

The Survey Helps to Pick the Best Professional Football Players

by Dave Michiels

As an Industrial Relations Consultant, Dave Michiels has been using the Survey for selection and development with great success for collegiate and professional football teams. *In the last five years, 90 percent of the NFL players drafted have been surveyed.*

Prior to the 1997 NFL Draft, Michiels completed Personal Surveys and individual interviews on more than four hundred players, compiling reports that identify and rank the fourteen different traits that scouts and coaches want to know about an athlete. By draft day, the teams using the Surveys have studied the reports in conjunction with their own information. Michiels says, "A lot of times, if the coach and scout differ on a choice, they will refer back to the Survey and then say, 'I'm going to go with yours.' They have that much confidence in it because they've seen the difference it can make."

"Coaches are becoming more aware of the character of the players and how it affects their potential for success. (Unfortunately, football develops *characters*, more than it develops character.) The scouts love it because it gives them a reliable tool that they didn't have before."

During his tenure as head football coach at Tulane University, Mack Brown gave credit to the Survey as "a very positive influence in our three-year turnaround of the

Tulane football program. I would recommend the testing as well as the counseling program to anyone in business who deals with people."

"I've done extensive research on testing over the years," Michiels reports. "The Survey is far superior to anything else on the market. The union says you cannot do psychological tests and the Survey is not a psychological test. It is the most objective character evaluation that I am aware of, and it has no racial implications or biases."

"One year I personally validated 132 surveys. I asked their coach, advisers, and people who knew them very well, "How accurate is this description?" All 132 were validated as accurate."

Among the professional teams who have used the Survey are the Miami Dolphins, New Orleans Saints, Green Bay Packers, and Dallas Cowboys. Collegiate teams include, among others, UCLA, Tulane, University of Oklahoma, and University of North Carolina.

Notes:

1. Richard F. Scheig, "Employee Turnover and Its Hidden Costs," *U.S. Distribution Journal* V224 n1 (Jan-Feb 1997), 14.

2. U.S. Bureau of Labor Statistics, "News Release," *Department of Labor,* USDL 84-86 (March 1, 1984).

3. R.A. Reilly and G.T. Chao, "Validity and Fairness of Some Alternative Selection Procedures," *Personnel Psychology* V35, 1982, 1-61.

4. John E. Hunter and Ronda F. Hunter, "Validity and Utility of Alternative Predictors of Job Performance," *Psychological Bulletin* V96, No. 1 (1984) 90.

Chapter 16

Developing Relationships and Emotional Intelligence

I n chapter 15, we discussed the absolute need every organization has for selecting and developing effective employees. In this chapter, we will discuss how to build relationships with others and how to develop emotional intelligence.

Like an X ray, the Simmons Personal Survey will let you immediately see which areas of a person's character are effective, which are too low, and which are too high. By knowing the person's strengths and weaknesses, you can see how to best relate to him or her, how to help that person grow, and how to help him or her get along better with others that person must work with. Then watch the person improve, do the job better, and even become ready for a position of higher responsibility.

Ways of Improving Relationships and Performance

1) Making Others Comfortable: In chapters 2 through 14, we discussed ways of developing compatibility between

two people. One way was to relate to people just as they are in such a way as to make them comfortable and to reduce conflict. This type of solution is practical when the person's character does not require change or when the person needs to change but refuses to do so.

For example, it may be acceptable for a particular worker to be hesitant (low self-direction). If so, give him: procedures, specific guidance, a plan to follow, help making decisions, much time to make decisions, confirmation of his decision—if he makes one, awareness of priorities, respect, and appreciation for following others' guidance. Get others to make decisions with or for him. He will normally want to be around a benevolent and capable leader.

2) Behavior Change: Still another solution offered in the earlier chapters involved managing behavior. Here certain things are emphasized, modeled, required, and rewarded. Other behaviors may receive discipline or punishment. Behavior management is called for when the person needs to change his or her behavior, but either is not willing to change his or her character or finds it difficult to get motivated to change it.

A person who needs to work more hours and stay on task may not buy into the idea of becoming more hardworking because it is so comfortable to be leisurely. Telling that person about all the neat counseling and self-help strategies may be of little interest to him. However, you can help to change his *behavior* if you tell him:

That eight hours of continuous, productive work are required and are necessary to receive full pay and privileges. (Or, if he does a type of work like raking leaves, he might be paid by the number of bags he fills.) He must start work at precisely 8:30 A.M. Break time is not until 10:00 A.M., etc. Standing around will receive a warning and a decrease in pay. If it happens twice, the penalty will be more severe. A third offense might result in termination.

Behavior management can often stimulate the proper *behavior*. However, if the person does not see the value and the correctness of the behavior, his *character* will not change. And when there is behavioral change without value change, there is much more stress involved. Therefore, it is still important to explain the reasons why certain things are and should be done. It is also important to be real and to model what you preach. While behavior management does not automatically result in true character change, it can be a good first step if there is no other way to get a person's cooperation.

3) Developing Emotional Intelligence (character): Another section in each chapter involves modifying personal tendencies. This solution is used when it is determined that the person really needs to make a personal change—when relating to the person in a manner that lets that person comfortably stay the way he or she is not practical. A manager who is compliant may need to develop assertiveness.

■ Ten Steps to Character Change

The following material will outline methods you can use to change character as indicated by the Personal Survey. This section will be written as if you will be helping another person make a change. However, you can also use the methods described for self-help.

1. The first step involved in making a character change is to become aware that some particular change is needed. This can be accomplished through an evaluation of the Personal Survey. Have the person take the Simmons Personal Survey and have the results sent to you.

2. When you discuss a person's Survey with her, it is important to mention her positive attributes first. This serves to make her less afraid of being seen as a total failure. And because there will be less threat, the person will not feel quite the need to be defensive with you. Then she can really consider the problems you mention. As you describe positive attributes, discuss examples of how this actually happens in her life. This will make the Survey results real to her and lay the groundwork for later discussion of problem areas.

3. If the person has a lot of problems, as indicated by the Survey, it is a good idea not to describe all of them at once, as this can be quite overwhelming and raise the person's defenses. Instead, only mention the most important areas needing improvement. As with positive areas, discuss real-life examples.

4. Once you have discussed each problem as outlined above, select one to work on first. Working on several difficulties at the same time is nearly impossible to do. Very serious problems that cause difficulty should receive first attention due to their possible harmful effects on the person or others around her.

5. After the first problem has been selected, you need to ensure that the person has the necessary motivation to overcome the problem. Very often what you see as being a problem will not be perceived as one to the person who has the problem. Even if the person understands that her attitude and/or behavior are not effective, she may have little desire to overcome them. To properly motivate a person, it can be very effective to show her what the consequences of continuing in the present pattern will be. Here you can, through dialogue, discuss all the limitations her behavior involves. For instance, some of the negative consequences of not being assertive may be: the strong chance of no promotion or raise in pay; the possibility of demotion, or even worse, being fired; always feeling compelled to agree even when you strongly disagree; getting manipulated by others, etc. Then you can show that person the advantages of changing. These are usually just the opposite of the disadvantages.

6. After Step 5 has been completed, ask her if she can see that it is to her advantage to make the change being discussed. Then check her degree of commitment to change. If she is properly committed, go to the next step of the process. If she is not, briefly remind her of the probable consequences of her actions. Again check the person's commitment, and if she still refuses to change, either select another area to work on or terminate the meeting.

7. Set a goal. This would normally involve selecting "solutions" from the corresponding section of this book. The goal is often the reverse of the problem. If a person is nonassertive, he needs to become more assertive. If he is

critical, he needs to stop criticizing and to compliment. If he avoids making decisions, he needs to begin making decisions. To ensure successful character change, goals that are far from the person's present level of behavior should be broken down into subgoals—small attainable steps. The steps gradually become more difficult or closer to the overall goal.

8. Some behaviors are so unfamiliar to the person that he needs to be shown how to do them. You may wish to train the person to do what you want and practice the response with him. As he practices the response, first mention what he did well and then point out what needs improvement.

9. When the person completes a step toward character change, it is beneficial for him to receive a reward for it as soon as possible. This will help make growth associated with reward. In this way, the person can actually change his emotional response toward growth in this area of character. Reinforcement can come in the form of money, material items, praise, recognition, and favored activities or privileges. The reward can be self-administered or given by others. It also may be useful to select a negative consequence to apply upon failure to complete a step or upon committing the problem behavior.

10. After a person has successfully met one major goal, then he can begin to work on others, one at a time. When the person has participated in a character-change program for a while (e.g., two to six months), readminister the Survey to objectively observe any character change.

The Ten Steps to Character Change mentioned above involve giving feedback to someone else or using information from the Survey to help you make personal changes. In the following section, one of our Associates, Bob Wall, shows how you can get others to give you valuable feedback. While this material is written as if a leader is receiving feedback from a subordinate, it can also involve getting feedback from peers.

How to Ask for Feedback

Taken from "Character in the Workplace: Observations from a Consultant's Point of View"
by Bob Wall Coauthor of The Visionary Leader

Most of us are poor observers of ourselves. We often have perceptions of ourselves that stand in marked contrast to how others see us. You may have recently received results from some form of 360-degree feedback process and need more information to understand how to make the necessary corrections. Or you may have taken the Simmons Survey and want to further investigate aspects of your character that might benefit from change. What follows is a structure for how to ask your staff and peers for feedback that will help you discover blind spots in your perception of yourself.

■ Preparing For the Conversation

Who to Ask

Pick two or three people who are most likely to speak frankly with you. Try to find people who are good observers and whose opinions you can trust. You should also seek out at least one person you think may have issues with you. You may learn something very useful about yourself, and your willingness to ask this person to give you feedback may help ease things between you. Also, seek out one or two peers, if you have some, who are in a good position to share perspectives with you.

■ Identifying Areas for Questions

You will find a number of questions to ask in the structure offered below. Write your own questions to get at issues of interest to you. If you have taken the Simmons Personal Survey, there are almost certainly areas that you will want to ask about. Be sure to ask about any characteristics that vary widely from the ideal score for your norm group. Ask for examples of how you might do what the Survey suggests you do (or fail to do). Also, ask about any Survey findings that you may disagree with. How do others see you with respect to this trait? Is the Survey accurate, at least at times, perhaps in ways that you yourself don't see clearly?

Leadership
....

What are the two or three things I do best as a leader?

What are two things I should do more often that would make me a better manager?

What are two things I should do less often that would make me a better manager?

Team Development

How can I do a better job of leading this team (department, company, etc.)?

What should I be doing more of to share my vision and goals for the team?

How can I do a better job of getting people involved in setting those goals?

What could I be doing to better represent the needs of this team to upper management?

What could I be doing to develop better teamwork with other teams?

Participation/Decision Making

In what areas do you need more authority for making decisions?

How can I make myself more available for your input on decisions I have to make?

What could I be doing to better share my own thinking about decisions I make?

List any examples of times when I am slow to make decisions.

How about instances when I make decisions too quickly or make decisions without enough consideration of how it affects people on this team?

Coaching

In what ways do I need to improve my attention to the performance of people on this team?

How can I improve in my response to good performance?

How can I improve in my response to poor performance?

Describe examples of poor performance that are not getting an appropriate response from me.

Conflict

In what ways do I need to do a better job of dealing with conflict on this team?

What are some ways that I might discourage people from expressing disagreements with me that really should be discussed?

What do I do that might be overly harsh or overly soft in dealing with conflict?

Cultural development

What do you like most about working on this team?

What do you like least about working on this team?

What needs to happen to make this a better place to work?

Interpersonal Qualities

Most leaders have qualities that people talk about with each other but not with the leader him/herself. When people talk about me, what complaints seem to come up from time to time?

What is the single most important thing you would like to see me do that would make me easier to work for and make this a better place for you to work?

■ Choosing the Setting

Schedule this conversation at a comfortable time in a comfortable place. Make sure that the other person has ample time and is not distracted by something else that needs to be done soon. Pick a setting that is comfortable for the other person. For example, if this person works for you, do not use your office. You have too many symbols of authority there. Go to the other person's office or, better yet, meet in a casual place such as a coffee shop away from work.

■ How to Behave During the Conversation

Most people are uncomfortable with feedback, whether they are giving it or receiving it. You are asking people to have a conversation with you that can provide you with valuable information. It is also a conversation that may make the other person uneasy, especially if you happen to be that person's manager. Your reaction to the feedback will have a lot to do with how open and detailed the other person will be in talking to you.

1) Remind yourself to be relaxed and casual. This conversation may in fact make you very nervous. Don't let it show. If you do, it may make the other person less willing to speak up honestly.

2) Establish your purpose. State that you have asked for some time because you want to ask for some feedback on how you are doing in your job as a leader (or fellow manager). Point out that most of us have things about ourselves that we don't see clearly and that you want the benefit of their perceptions, especially regarding things you can do to improve.

3) Put the other person at ease. Point out that you are aware that this kind of conversation doesn't happen very often. (This is especially true when you are talking to someone who reports to you—most feedback goes the other way, from you to them.) Assure that person that you want him or her to be open with you, that you very much want to hear what that person has to say.

Self-disclosure can be disarming but only if it is genuine. For example, if you are yourself uncomfortable about this conversation, say so. "I don't know about you but conversations like this sometimes make me a little uneasy because I'm not quite sure what I am going to hear. Nevertheless, I promise to do my best to listen." Imagine how you might feel if your own boss asked you for feedback and talk about that: "I was thinking about how I would feel if my boss asked me for feedback. I realized that you might feel a little uneasy about me asking you these kinds of questions."

4) Explore areas of interest to you. Proceed to ask questions, exploring the suggested topics. Add your own questions to make certain that you get at information vital to you. Take notes.

5) Listen. Listen. Listen. You are asking for information. Listen to what the other person is saying. Stay focused on the other person, not your internal commentary on what you are hearing. To make sure you understand, paraphrase what you are hearing. Stating in your own words what you think the other person is saying is a great way to clarify any distortions in your own listening. Make certain that you fully understand the feedback and do not leave with any misunderstandings.

6) Ask questions that require a detailed response. The questions in the suggested structure for the conversation have been carefully phrased to elicit information. For example, don't ask "Is there anything that I do that makes me difficult to disagree with?" If the other person is uncomfortable with this question, it is very easy to evade the topic by saying, "No. Not at all."

Consequently, I have phrased all the questions in a way that leaves less "wiggle room" and is more likely to generate useful information. Phrase questions like this: "What are two or three things I do that may at times make me difficult to disagree with?" Before writing your own questions to supplement those found in the suggested structure, be sure to study how I have phrased the questions and phrase your own in a similar way.

7) Do not defend yourself. If you start offering excuses or examples that contradict the other person, that person is likely to shut down and stop offering information. He or she didn't agree to this conversation to get into an argument with you. You have asked that person to share his or her perceptions of you. Give that person the courtesy of listening. Remind yourself that even if you disagree with that person's perception, it is still his or her perception. The most important thing for you to remember is that in some instances perception is reality. When you hear something that is surprising or is not consistent with your own perception of yourself, there is probably something that you are doing—or not doing—that contributes to the other person's perception of you. Find out as much as you can so that you can begin to behave in a way that will have people see you the way you want to be seen.

8) Ask for examples to clarify broad generalizations. If the other person uses words that are open to interpretation, ask for more specific information. If, for example, the other person says something like "At times you are rude" or "I wish you weren't so hard to talk to," ask for more specific information to understand what he means. Ask follow-up questions such as, "I really want to understand what you are saying. Is there something I do or fail to do that gives you that impression? Is it my tone of voice? Is it an expression on my face that I might not be aware of? Is there something I say that leaves you with this feeling about me? Can you think of a time recently that is a good example of what you are talking about?"

9) Take action. If feedback is accurate and apologies are in order, apologize. See if the two of you can reach an agreement on how to handle similar situations in the future.

On the other hand, you may wish to think about what has been said. You are under no obligation to respond to everything that has been said immediately. Tell the person that you appreciate his or her willingness to talk to you and that he or she has given you a lot to think about. If a follow-up conversation is appropriate, promise to get back to him or her. Then make sure that you do just that.

Even if some of the feedback seems off the mark, do not get defensive. You can always say something like, "You have described me in some ways that surprise me. They don't fit my concept of myself at all. But I promise you that I will think about what you have said and observe myself more closely in the future. I would also appreciate it if you would call this to my attention if you see me doing the same thing in the future. Most of us have things we do out of habit, and I may be doing this without any awareness of how it affects people around me, and you may be able to help me see it more clearly."

10) Close the conversation. Thank the person for his or her willingness to talk openly with you and assure him or her that you will carefully consider what he or she had to say. Let them know that you are open to this kind of feedback at any time and look forward to addressing areas you are learning about from them and from others.

Personal Development and Team-Building Success Stories

Ongoing Personal Development

Wes Crane, Human Resource Consultant

We're working with a seafood company in Alaska. One of the managers aboard one of the processing ships had a Survey that was more toward the worker profile. He had been promoted into a very strong leader role and *was* being successful, but was under much stress.

When we approached him with the Survey and showed him the areas that needed improving for him to move up in the company or even to be comfortable as a leader, he took that on as a challenge to make it happen.

Here is a case where a young man knew that to be successful and to move up he had to be uncomfortable with where he was and had to make change. He dug right in the next day. His boss would call me on occasion and say, "You just would not believe what this guy is doing." He began reading self-help books and leadership books all on his own. In a conversation with him later, I found that he did a lot of self-talk. He looked at his own behaviors while he was handling people in different situations.

Over the next two years he took the Survey a couple of different times as a measuring device to see how he was doing. Every Survey that we measured him on showed an increase in leadership traits.

The key was his response to his first Survey results. He realized that he wanted to be more, to do more, and was going to have to *change character* to do it. Upon accepting that, he set about doing everything he could to start building a stronger character.

Over a two-year period, he went from a good worker up to a very well-adjusted middle executive. That was about five years ago, and now he is very successful, in charge of all the production of the boat. He has made lasting change now.

Job Success Follows a Conscious Decision to Grow

Doug Jones, Management Consultant

One of my first clients as a consultant was a family-owned grocery wholesale company in the mid-South. This company, LaLa Foods (we will call it) also operated about ten company stores as well as servicing mountain stores, both large and small. My assignment was to begin to reorganize and upgrade management for more improved store profitability and image.

One particular individual stood out in my mind and was a source of some satisfaction for me personally. Matt (not his name) was an assistant manager, actually a glorified stock boy. Matt's Survey revealed he had a relatively moderate emotional energy level, basically a team member, not a leader at all. He was not identified as someone to watch for future promotion.

About a year later, I began to get feedback that Matt had made a terrific turnabout, had become a dynamic force in his store, often surpassing and outperforming his store manager. Though somewhat skeptical at the seeming "transformation," I agreed to retest Matt to see if, in fact, he had actually achieved personal growth.

The results were shocking and undeniable. Matt had shown significant personal growth in all areas of character that would be associated with an effective leader. Based on his actual performance and Survey results, I recommended his promotion to manager.

While at his store one day, I asked Matt what or who had been responsible for his turnaround. His reply was that I was responsible. Though flattered, I asked that he be more specific.

Matt basically said that when he saw his original Survey results, he was not happy with the individual I had identified him to be, and he wanted to make a change. He took charge of his own personal growth, made a conscious decision to accept the risks associated with leadership, and grew as a person. Matt continues to be one of the top managers in the group at this writing.

Measuring Character Can Be the Basis for a Complete Management Process

Keith Floto, Human Resource Consultant

The Survey's tremendous value has been in its use in both selection and team-building. The restaurant business traditionally has an incredibly high turnover rate industry-wide. The Survey really pinpointed those characteristics important for success.

Selection: I was a human resource consultant for a large Wendy's franchise. Their fifty-seven stores were experiencing a turnover rate of 50 to 100 percent in management. While courses in better interviewing techniques had been helpful, they were not enough to tell us who we were dealing with in the interview.

Many applicants present themselves as enthusiastic, hard workers—"I'm a workaholic. I'm not afraid to work hard and put in long hours." But the Survey would tell you whether that was real or not. Having a dependable way to identify their commitment to work, positive attitude, emotional energy, and decision-making levels helped us choose managers who were right for our situation. The Survey was a vital part of our hiring process for management positions.

Training: The Survey was used not so much to eliminate a person from the hire but to enable us to put together a development plan for him or her. From the Survey, we could tell the training manager, "These are the things you're going to see in his or her work. This is how you can help him or her grow." The trainee and the supervisor were then working together toward the same goals.

Developing better managers meant they stayed longer, were more effective, and felt better about their jobs. The bottom line was we not only lowered our expenses by reducing turnover, we also increased sales with better-trained managers.

Team-Building: The results of a six-month pilot study completely validated the importance of using the Survey for team-building.

Forty stores were divided into two groups, with careful attention to balance in all market factors. Group one followed the franchise's well-established training procedures without using the Survey.

All managers and trainees in group two were given the Simmons Personal Survey at the beginning of the study. Each one had the opportunity to go over his or her Survey evaluation with his or her supervisor and work up a personal development plan. A follow-up Survey was done three months later with improvements recognized and development plans reviewed.

After six months, stores using the Simmons Survey for team-building had improved significantly more than the other stores in all three areas tracked: 1) Sales Increase up 10 percent; 2) Quality Service And Cleanliness Inspection improved a full grade level; 3) Crew Turnover Rate reduced. Overall profitability had improved as well.

Some people are intimidated by taking tests in general and by the Survey in particular—initially, because it is *so* accurate. But once they understand how it is used to *help* them, they realize there's no risk to taking it. The Survey really helped the supervisor build teamwork, with everyone drawing off each other's strengths and supporting them in the areas they need to work on. As an employer, we saw we *had* to have it.

The Survey Gives Awareness That Frees Us to Make Change

Jerry Turk, Management Consultant

I recently used the Survey with the entire management team of a bank. It was very effective in pulling people together, talking openly about their lesser strengths. By allowing the Survey to identify them, we were able to confront some interpersonal relationships that were deteriorating and effectively mend those relationships.

All but one of the team members responded positively. One very inflexible member could not be brought around and was later replaced. However, several senior managers were able to acknowledge their problems. They took the attitude of "I can work on that," which allowed them to resolve specific problems. It resulted in better teamwork with more interpersonal cooperation between departments.

One member of the team was an executive vice president who was hesitant to follow through with difficult decisions. He very capably made policy decisions but then wouldn't stick to his guns, wouldn't carry them out. He wanted to be liked by everyone and had a very difficult time in taking a firm stance when it was required. With the Survey test data to support what was actually taking place, other team members had the courage to step forward and say, "Yes, this is our observation, too, and it's causing us serious problems."

As we talked to him, he began to recognize that this was a pattern in his life that he could change. He was able to become more aware of when this was occurring and was willing to deal with it. The Survey helped him to break out of immobility, make a decision, and take positive action.

The Simmons Personal Survey The Ultimate Tool for Measuring Emotional Intelligence

Now that you know what you can learn by measuring emotional intelligence, you may be wondering, "What exactly is the Simmons Personal Survey?" It is an in-depth, character assessment tool, quickly and easily administered to individuals by pencil-and-paper form or on-screen with computer or Internet versions.

Administration and Scoring: The Survey is administered in two parts. On Part I, persons check any of 360 adjectives, stating how they think others feel about them. On Part II, they check any of 360 adjectives that describe how they feel about themselves. Subjects may refer to an adjective dictionary (written at a sixth-grade reading level) to understand any unfamiliar words.

The Adjective Advantage: Adjectives are used instead of the long sentences that most other tests use for two important reasons.

1) Single adjectives such as the word "responsible" are easily understood and can be responded to quickly. Using
adjectives allows the Survey to have a very reliable data-
base (720 responses) *and* a very low average completion
time (just thirty minutes)!

2) Second, checking adjectives gives the subject less ability
to control how his or her results look, yielding a more
honest response more often.

Two Tests in One: Instead of merely letting the subject say how he
sees himself, the Survey balances this information against the
person's perception of how others see him. This method of using
the perception of "others" is a proven interviewing technique.

For instance, if a manager is asked "How considerate are
you of your workers?" he will usually say, "I am very considerate." He may even be able to give you a few examples of times
when he has been considerate.

However, when asked "How considerate do your workers
think you are?" we often get a quite different answer. They
may say, "They think I am too harsh." When asked "Why do
these workers feel you are harsh?" we begin to see examples of
harshness, often to the surprise of the interviewee.

Character tests that leave out this "other" information cannot possibly achieve the accuracy of the Personal Survey,
since they rely solely upon the person's "self-concept," which
is only half of the picture at best.

■ Results

Using the 720 responses, the Survey makes almost two thousand individual computer measurements and cross-compar-

isons. This results in thirteen scales, which measure the subject's typical or usual commitment to perform in a certain manner.

Validity Indicators: Every Personal Survey goes through five validity checks to ensure that the results are valid, ruling out inappropriate test-taking behavior such as random answering, faking good, faking bad, secrecy, excessive confusion, unrealistic self-concepts, etc.

Norms that Predict Success: Studies were conducted to determine which characteristics were associated with success in a given job category—and which characteristics were associated with failure.

Persons who were top performers in their job category were surveyed. Poor performers in the same job categories were also surveyed. It was found that the scores of top performers were very similar to each other and very different from the scores of poor performers.

These score patterns became our job norms, giving the Survey the ability to compare a person's character to a wide variety of job environments and to predict the level of performance.

Our standard norms include: The Well-adjusted Person, General Laborer, Skilled Laborer, Rugged Laborer, Detailed Worker, Relational Detailed Worker, Analyst, Practitioner, Creative/Artist, Manager/Instructor, Executive, Top Executive, and Sales Norms.

Custom Norms: We provide a one-page form that will allow you to easily make a custom job norm in five to ten minutes. This form will allow you to tell us what you want and don't want in an employee. The norm will then be used with our reports and graphs enabling them to identify persons who are best qualified for a given job.

You can base your responses upon what you know about the job requirements. *Or,* you can use the actual Survey scores of your top performers and of your poor performers, giving you a validated custom norm. This will allow you to "reproduce" the best employees.

Turnaround time for the Simmons Personal Survey is usually just fifteen minutes by fax, on the Internet, or by mail.

■ Proven to Work

Uniquely Validated: The Survey was originally validated using an intensive case-study method. Extensive background information was gathered on each person surveyed. Then this information was compared to Survey scores. If a discrepancy occurred, the computations were adjusted so that the scores would match the person.

This process was conducted with hundreds of subjects, varying in age, sex, race, education, and job position. Instead of making people fit the Survey, the Survey was made to fit people.

Highly Valid: The Survey has been rated by our clients as being from 95 to 100 percent accurate. That is, when we say someone is a very hard worker, they are. If we say someone is pushy and overbearing, they are.

We have also done studies to compare the overall success of employees on their jobs with their scores on the Personal Survey.

At a large Wendy's franchise. the Survey was found to correlate .86 with the job performance of restaurant managers, as measured by the company's semiannual performance review.

At Olsten's Temporary Services, the Survey correlated a perfect 1.00 with the job performance of its sales force, as measured by the company's Presidents Club Ranking.

At Methodist Hospitals, the Survey correlated .68 with the job performance of hospital nurses, as measured by the Methodist Hospitals Performance Appraisal.

Realize that because other factors such as intelligence, job training, physical strength, etc., also influence job performance, no single measurement could hope to achieve a perfect 1.00 correlation. Most tests achieve no more than a .40 correlation with total job performance.

Highly Reliable: The average test-retest reliability correlation is .74, which is considered to be a high degree of correlation.

Legal and Safe: The Personal Survey, when used in accordance with our established methods, involves virtually no legal risk. The Survey has no adverse impact on any group and can be used within EEOC guidelines!

Since 1975, when the Personal Survey was first used, only two lawsuits have involved the Survey in any way. On both occasions, the case was dropped, and no fault was found with the Survey.

The Survey has been effectively and safely used in thousands of organizations all over the United States since 1975—in industrial settings, restaurants, hotel chains, grocery stores, retail stores, hospitals, schools, sports teams, banks, churches, etc.

Consider also that effective hiring cuts down on lawsuits related to firing employees. According to a research report in the Stanford Law Review, there are six times as many lawsuits involving termination as there are for not hiring an applicant.

■ We Have an Opportunity for You

Thanks for reading our book. I trust that it has been very helpful to you. While much has been shared with you in this book, there is an opportunity for even more help through pursuing one of the opportunities listed below.

1. To help you to quickly see the value of measuring your emotional intelligence on a scale, you can do the Brief Self Examination of Emotional Intelligence found on page 318 and 319. This self exam demonstrates how emotional intelligence varies by degree, and makes the point that your EQ should match the job you do and the people you relate to.

2. You can accurately assess your own emotional intelligence for personal growth, career guidance and marital compatibility, by taking the EQ Profile or EQ Insights as discussed in Section II.

3. You can use the Survey for character assessment in your business personnel procedures such as hiring, training, employee development, team building, career pathing, etc. To find out how to get started, mail the attached response card* to an authorized SMS Associate.

The Simmons Personal Survey is sold through a nationwide network of independent consultants, authorized as Associates of Simmons Management Systems (SMS). They will help you match your assessment and budget needs to the wide range of reports and graphs available to businesses. A chart of Associates who may be contacted by the mail-in response card is included here for your convenience. Specific areas of consulting services also available are listed in the chart.

4. If you are a Consultant or Counselor, you can provide the Simmons Personal Survey to your clients for their personal and business assessment needs. Contact an Associate marked in Column B of the Associate chart for information on becoming an authorized SMS Associate.

> **Note:** Pricing and services vary among Associates. If you would like to contact more than one Associate, or if the mail-in reponse card is missing, write the following information on a piece of paper: Your name, company name, street address, city, state, zip, phone number and fax number.

Brief Self Examination of Emotional Intelligence (Character)

Below is a very brief summary of the scales that are used in the Simmons Personal Survey. For each scale, try to determine if you are low, moderate, high, or very high. Write your first initial in the box that most sounds like you. Then write a "J" in the box that describes what your job calls for. You can also place the first initial of someone you relate to (e.g. your boss or spouse) in the box that best describes them. If the "J" is in a different box than your initial, write the letter "J" to the right of the scale followed by a number like 1 or 2 depending on how many boxes apart the "J" is from your initial. Do the same thing in comparing your score to the score of the person you relate to. Areas

	Low	Moderate
Slow Paced	Slow. Inactive. Tires Easily.	Moderate pace and moderate activity.
Relaxed	Calm and complacent.	Low stress.
Faultfinding	Sees problems. Fault Finding.	Moderately positive attitude.
Humble	Modest. Self Critical.	Moderate self esteem.
Leisurely	Rests or plays.	Moderate work.
Spontaneous	Spontaneous. Careless.	Moderate attention to detail.
Routine	Likes routine, sameness and repetition.	Moderate tendency to change things.
Cautious	Likes security, safety and comfort.	Moderate courage.
Hesitant	Guided by others.	Prefers advice.
Compliant	Cooperative, compliant non-assertive.	Moderately assertive.
Intolerant	Rejects abuse. Angers easily.	Moderately patient.
Self Willed	Takes care of own needs. Selfish.	Moderately caring.
Reserved	Enjoys being alone. Reserved.	Likes to work or be with a few familiar people.

that are marked "J1" are causes of significant job problems. "J2" is a serious problem and "J3" is very serious. The same is true for the relationship scores you calculated. For more help, see the corresponding chapters in our book. Please note that only the Simmons Personal Survey can provide a precise and thorough evaluation of your character. We caution against making personal, job, or relational decisions on the basis of this brief self-examination. We strongly recommend that you look at the inside back cover of the book and order one or more Personal Survey answer blanks.

High	**Very High**	
Fast and active	Very fast and hyperactive.	**Fast Paced**
Moderate stress.	Under excessive stress.	**Stressed**
Positive attitude. Cheerful.	Carefree/ Naive.	**Positive**
Likes self.	Prideful. Defensive.	**Self Assured**
Works much.	Compelled to Work.	**Hard Working**
Careful and precise.	Perfectionist. Compulsive about details.	**Careful**
Enjoys new ideas, places, things and behavior.	Compelled to change things. Bored with the same thing.	**Changing**
Faces discomfort, pressure, and danger to reach a goal.	Very brave. Takes large risks.	**Courageous**
Problem solves.	Decides, but controls decisions.	**Decisive**
Asserts opinions. Can demand.	Asserts and pushes. Dominating.	**Assertive**
Slow to anger.	Tolerant. Denies anger.	**Tolerant**
Helpful and honest.	Helps. Sacrifices own needs.	**Considerate.**
Outgoing. Meets and greets.	Meets and greets. Verbose.	**Sociable.**

■ Simmons Personal Survey Providers

To receive further information about the Survey in business applications, including ordering, pricing, and services available, complete the attached response card and mail or fax it to a Simmons Associate. The chart provides an alphabetical list of participating independent consultants, along with the following information:

Column A. Consulting Servies

These columns indicate the specific areas of service the Associate provides for Survey application: Employee Selection, Training and Team Building, Employee Personal Growth, Employee Career Pathing, and Outplacement. Each Associate is experienced in using the Survey to meet your organizational needs, including initial implementation, training and support in these areas.

Column B. Associate Marketing Information

If you are a Consultant or Counselor, you may be interested in providing the Simmons Personal Survey to your clients. Contact an Associate marked in this column for information on becoming an authorized SMS Associate.

Associate Specialty and Location

Each independent Associate offers a unique range of consulting services and expertise which may be of value to you in your business. A brief summary of their services is provided with examples of their client base, and the location in which their consulting services are available. Detailed information is available from the Associate on request.

Simmons Personal Survey Provider

	SELECTION	TRAINING	EMPL. GROWTH	CAREER PATH	OUTPLACE	ASSOC. INFO
			A			B
Mr. Bill Bainbridge **The Witan Group, Inc.** P.O. Box 1188, Prairie Grove, AR. 72744	•	•	•	•	•	•
Mr. John Beane **Leadership Concepts** P. O. Box 700, China Grove, NC 28023-0778 Fax: (704) 857-5566 E-mail:jbeane2@prodigy.net	•	•	•			•
Ms Barbara Bender **Bender, Inc.** 6 Pineway Court, Little Rock, AR 72211	•	•	•			•
Mr. Wesley Crane **Second Opinion** 4501 Shilshole Ave., N.W., Seattle, WA 98107 Fax (206) 783-6885	•	•	•	•		•
Dr. John T. Johnson, Ph.D. **Personal Management Consultants** 907 Tusculum Blvd. Greeneville, TN 37745 Fax: (423) 638-3466	•	•	•	•	•	•
Mr. Doug Jones **Doug Jones & Associates** 3572 Salisbury Drive Lexington, KY 40510 Fax: (606) 255-9716	•	•	•	•		•
Charles T. Kenny, Ph.D. **Kenny & Associates, Inc.** 5824 Garden River Cove Memphis, TN 38120 Fax: (901) 682-0455 E-mail: ctkkenny@aol.com	•	•	•	•	•	•
Mrs. Leslie Malin **Management By Design** 401 Great Neck Road, Glen Cove, NY 11021 Fax: (516) 466-8636	•	•	•	•	•	

Organizational development and marketing consulting: personnel and management team assessment, Employee Feelings Inventory. General business, industrial and industry /US

Human resource consulting: self-directed work teams, problem solving, effective communications, personal productivity, results-oriented training. Speaker, trainer, seminar leader. Offers business surveys over the Internet worldwide. Manufacturing, industrial, construction, business and professional organizations. /International

Consulting in human resources, training and development. Offers businesses the ability to take the Survey over the Internet worldwide. Manufacturing, Banking, Industrial ./International

Human resource consulting: coordinated strategies for efficient personnel development, reducing turnover and employee costs while building strong management teams. Employee Feelings Inventory. Retail food and furniture chains, churches, airlines, manufacturing, colleges, transportation, seafood processing, construction, entertainment, marketing, Native Alaskan business and organizations./International

Management consulting. Management and supervisory training, executive search and recruitment. Employee Feelings Inventories. Hospitals, health care, educational, manufacturing, advertising, printing, insurance, aviation, utilities. /US

Organizational analysis, leadership study, team building, marketing and consumer studies, system's automation, human resources Consulting, Employee Feelings Inventory. Retail/Wholesale grocery, Educational inst., franchise restaurants, manufacturing. /US

The Right Brain People.®, Psychology-based analytical consulting for Fortune 500 clients. Market Research Consumer Psychology, In-Sight interviewing, validation studies. Seminars on key management issues. Manufacturing, hospitals/health care, property management, automobile industry. /US

Preemployment assessment. Career development assessment, training, one-on-one coaching. Employment agencies, Retail sales /Northeast US

Simmons Personal Survey Provider

	Selection	Training	Empl. Growth (A)	Career Path (A)	Outplace	Assoc. Info (B)
Mr. Dave Michiels **David Michiels & Associates** P.O. Box 640027, Kenner, LA 70064 Fax: (504) 586-8248 E-mail: chef@arcadmia.net	•	•	•			
Ms. Maria Ort **Duckmint Partnership, Inc.** P. O. Box 30390, Phoenix, AZ 85046 Fax:(602)266-4433 E-mail: ptnrsmrt@primenet.com www.primenet.com/nptnrsmrt	•	•	•	•	•	
Mr. Patrick Sumpter **Operations Consultants Co., Inc.** 2014 N.W. Douglas Street, Camas, WA 98607 Fax: (360) 910-6064 E-mail:psumpocc@aol.com	•	•	•	•		•
Mr. Paul Tomlinson **Career/Life Institute** 18761 58th Avenue N.E., Seattle, WA 98155 Fax: (425) 646-7601	•	•		•	•	
Touchstone Consulting, Inc. 835 East Lamar Blvd., Suite 186, Arlington, TX 76011 Fax: (817) 459-1748	•	•	•	•		•
Mr. Charles Tull **CLT Associates** #10 Pinnacle Point, Little Rock, AR 72205 E-mail: lctull@arkasas.net	•	•				
Ms. Regina Brumfield **Strategic Partners** 705 Heaven's Drive, #5, Mandeville, LA 70471 Fax: (504) 854-2518	•	•	•			•
~~**Mr. Bob Wall**~~ **Bob Wall & Associates** 2737 37th Ave., S.W., Seattle, WA 98126 Fax: (206) 938-3094 E-mail: bobwall@nwlink.com	•	•	•	•		•

Industrial relations consulting and counseling: Establishing criteria for personal and team success, structured goal setting for developing individual potential, coordinated selection and training. Professional and collegiate athletic teams, national sports associations, government and educational institutions, entertainment management. /US

Synergistic Partnering: preventing and repairing problems in partnership relationships and team management in business, industry, government and educational agencies. Creator of Partner $mart Programs®; Author, *The Significant 7 - Key Issues In Business Partnership*; Speaker, Trainer and Group Facilitator. /US

Personnel assessment, labor scheduling, and time management, general business and retail grocery consulting. Business brokerage and entrepreneurial assessment. /Pacific Northwest, Southwest US, and Canada

Personal assessment and career pathing. Nonprofit organizations, educational institutions, hospitals, manufacturing, and privately held companies /Northwest US

Management consulting and human resource development. Food service, health care, and manufacturing inductries. /US

Business brokerage. /US

Organizational consulting in the financial industry: Evaluation of structure, forms and systems design for sales and service. Coordinated team building with individual assessment and Employee Feelings Inventory. Bank, Credit Union, Savings and Loan, general business /US and Canada

Corporate "snap-shot," individual and team assessment to identify leadership strengths and weaknesses, relationship problems. Management development training to increase individual and corporate effectiveness. Author of *The Visionary Leader*, Speaker, Trainer. Gov't and educ. inst., manufacturing, medical/ health, insurance, communications, transportation, grocery, legal, banking /International.

Your Opportunity To Take The Next Step!

You've learned the importance of emotional intelligence to your personal success and you've seen how accurate measurement of character traits provide the key to growth and change. Now you're ready to take action! Take advantage of the two opportunities offered below:

Card A - FOR INDIVIDUALS: Order your choice of the self-awareness versions of the Simmons Personal Survey for yourself and your family members (18 years or above). *If Card A has been removed, you may write to Simmons Management Systems, P.O. Box 770265, Memphis, TN 38117-0265.*

Card B - FOR BUSINESS: Find out how the business versions of The Simmons Personal Survey can help you successfully place and develop employees, raise productivity and cut employee costs. Send Card B to an authorized SMS Associate. (See Appendix for listing.) *If Card B has been removed, you may write to one of the Associates listed in the Appendix.* **You can also find us on the Internet at www.eqhelp.com.**

- -

Card A: Use this card to order Surveys for individual self-awareness, to develop personal strengths, build relationships and success in your career. Neatly print the following:

Name _____ Occupation_____
Street Address_____ Phone (____)_____ Fax (____)_____
City _____ ST _____ Zip _____ E-mail Address _____

Choose what you want and how you want to pay:

__ **EQ Insights** @ $19.95 each $_____
A two page report with brief evaluations of all 13 areas of character and general recommendations.

__ **EQ Profile** @ $75.00 each $_____
EQ Insights plus a detailed graph showing the exact level of each tendency, the full range of feelings and behavior, the direction the tendencies are moving, and rankings for 13 job norms.

TOTAL $_____

Method of Payment   __ Visa   __ Mastercard   __Cashier's Check   __ Money Order

__ __ __ __ __ __ __ __ __ __ __ __ __ __ __ __ __ / __ __

Credit Card Account Number   Expiration Date

Signature _____

Mail this card (in an envelope) with your payment to Simmons Management Systems, P.O. Box 770265, Memphis, TN 38117-0265. You will receive your Survey answer blank(s) with instructions for processing. Please allow 10-14 days for delivery.

- -

Card B: Use this card if you want to use the Survey in a business setting. *Put the power of Measuring Emotional Intelligence to work in your business.* **Neatly print the following:**

Name _____Position _____
Company Name _____ Type of Business _____
Street Address_____ Phone (____)_____ Fax (____)_____
City _____ ST _____ Zip _____ E-mail Address _____

Mark all areas of interest:

__ Employee Selection __Training __Team Building
__ Personal Growth __Employee Attitude Survey __Career Pathing __Outplacement
__ Other:_____
__ To become an SMS Associate (For Business Consultants and Counselors only)

Mail this card (in an envelope) to an Authorized SMS Associate from the list provided.